SAS AND ELITE FORCES GUIDE
PRISONER
ESCAPE & EVASION

SAS AND ELITE FORCES GUIDE
PRISONER OF WAR ESCAPE & EVASION

HOW TO SURVIVE BEHIND ENEMY LINES FROM THE WORLD'S ELITE MILITARY UNITS

CHRIS McNAB

LYONS PRESS
Guilford, Connecticut

An imprint of Globe Pequot Press

Copyright © 2012 Amber Books Ltd
All illustrations © Amber Books Ltd
Published by Amber Books Ltd (www.amberbooks.co.uk)

This Lyons Press edition first published in 2012

Lyons Press is an imprint of Globe Pequot Press.

Library of Congress Cataloging-in-Publication Data is available on file.

ISBN: 978-0-7627-7989-5

Project editor: Michael Spilling
Design: Brian Rust
Illustrations: Tony Randell

Printed in Singapore

10 9 8 7 6 5 4 3 2 1

DISCLAIMER
This book is for information purposes only. Readers should be aware of the legal position in
their country of residence before practicing any of the techniques described in this book.
Neither the author nor the publisher can accept responsibility for any loss, injury, or damage
caused as a result of the use of the combat techniques described in this book, nor for any
prosecutions or proceedings brought or instigated against any person or body that may result
from using these techniques.

CONTENTS

INTRODUCTION

Throughout the history of warfare, literally millions of men and women have found themselves prisoners of the enemy. Whether captured in their thousands during an open battle, or snatched individually by a terrorist group, they have faced one of the most unsettling of human experiences. Their lives depend on the mercy of their captors, and if they find that mercy in short supply, then captivity can become a brute struggle for survival. Some 5.7 million Soviets were taken prisoner by the

Isolation

Being held prisoner, either by terrorists or by conventional forces, is a bewildering experience, producing emotions of loneliness, fear, uncertainty, helplessness and despair. A strong will to survive is essential.

Germans during World War II, for example, but 3.3 million of them died in the ghastly Nazi camps.

One of the most terrifying aspects of captivity is that a prisoner no longer has control over his own destiny, or even his most basic human activities, such as eating or drinking. He is also prey to casual sadism, or to outright and systematic torture, at any time, day or night. The result can be a sense of utter helplessness and futility. Yet throughout history, across the countless years of warfare, there have always been those prisoners of war (POWs) who refuse to submit to their chains, and who from the outset set their minds on escape.

Trying to find a psychological ingredient common to such people is not easy, as they come from all walks of life and social classes. Their motivation to escape is also varied – some burn with the desire to see their families again; others want to return to the fight; many POWs get bored and treat escape as a form of intellectual exercise; some simply fear that if they don't escape, they will be die in captivity. What emerges from such motivations, and many others, is an abiding commitment to be free, with individuals committing every mental and physical resource to that goal.

Trained to Escape

This book is in part about the strategies, skills and techniques of escaping from enemy captivity, whether in the context of a POW camp or of a terrorist cell. Yet it is also about how to stay free in the first place, the ability to evade pursuers when isolated behind enemy lines. The content of this book

Constant Observation

From the very first moment he enters captivity, bound and restrained, this well-trained soldier memorizes as much as can about his surroundings. Such information may come in useful later on during an escape attempt.

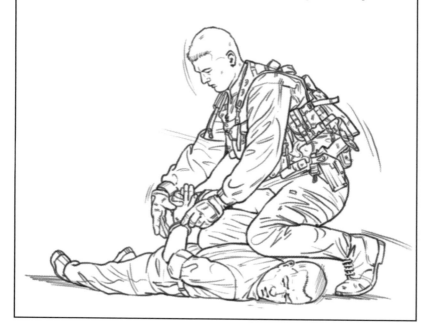

has benefited from the explosion of research from the mid-twentieth century into what the US military now terms 'SERE' – Survival, Evasion, Resistance, Escape – much of which has been distilled into officially distributed manuals. It also utilizes the practical experience of numerous evaders and escaped POWs, whose narratives punctuate the practical instruction given here.

What emerges from such sources is that the successful evader is typically someone capable of clear

Vigilance

Successful escape and evasion depends heavily upon vigilance. The soldier must use all his senses to the maximum, to detect emerging threats and changes in the survival situation.

thought in even the most stressful of circumstances. Fear can rarely be suppressed entirely, but proper training and a defiant mindset can push it to the back of consciousness so that an individual can function even under intense pressure. Furthermore, a soldier on the run must adopt both optimism and realism in equal measures. Optimism is the sense that both escape and evasion are achievable goals, no matter how bleak the surroundings. Realism, however, scrutinizes plans and actions with a dispassionate eye, assessing them coldly and rationally to judge their chances of success.

US survival and SERE manuals have distilled a useful 'SURVIVAL' mnemonic to remember some of the core principles of how to keep one step ahead of the enemy:

> **S** – Size up the situation.
> Physical condition
> Adequate water intake
> Injuries, Illness
> Food
> Surroundings
> Equipment
> **U** – Use all your senses, slow down and think.
> **R** – Remember where you are.
> **V** – Vanquish fear and panic.
> **I** – Improvise and improve.
> **V** – Value living.
> **A** – Act like the natives.
> **L** – Live by your training and experience.

The list balances nicely between the poles of optimism and realism mentioned above. What it implicitly reiterates in each point is that every action needs to be considered before being implemented. Never strike out blindly for freedom without thought of where you are going, how you might get there, and how you will survive on the way. You could get lucky and evade recapture or

Endurance

Escape and evasion is typically a physically arduous experience. Prepare to be cold, wet and tired, but also never ignore serious physical symptoms developing. Always remember your key priorities – water, food and shelter – regardless of how tough you regard yourself to be.

death, but the history of escape and evasion illustrates how the odds may be stacked against even the most prepared of special forces soldiers. For this reason, an evader needs to make all actions contribute in a meaningful way to getting home.

This book also makes no bones about the fact that escape and evasion are difficult, especially when trying to defeat an enemy who is using all of his intellectual, natural and technical resources to keep you imprisoned or track you down. Yet it does show how the very fact of being pursued, or of being held in captivity, does not reduce you to the status of a helpless pawn. Indeed, with a bit of knowledge, a lot of courage, and an ability to think laterally, you stand a good chance of making it home.

Although most modern military forces provide training in prisoner of war (POW) survival, it is obviously far more advisable to avoid capture in the first place. The conditions in which soldiers are likely to fall prisoner change according to the nature of the conflict. During major set-piece battles, such as those which took place during World War II, soldiers are most likely to be captured *en masse* when their unit is outmanoeuvred or outfought by the enemy. In June 1941, for example, some 287,000 Soviet soldiers became prisoners after they were encircled by the German Army Group Centre during the battle of Bialystok–Minsk, just one of several strategic disasters that threatened to overwhelm the Soviet Union during Operation *Barbarossa*. No conflict since 1945 has matched World War II for its scale of captives, but the Indochina War (1945–54), Vietnam War (1963–75), Indo–Pakistan War (1971), Iran–Iraq War (1980–88) and the 1991 Gulf War all saw substantial prisoner counts following conventional engagements.

On an individual level, there is often little a soldier can do to prevent

. . . .

Hiding and evading is a test of nerve, intelligence and skil, and demands a high level of mental stamina. The central point is to consider the implications of every action before making it.

All escape and evasion is a battle of minds, yours against your opponent's. Try to imagine yourself in the enemy's position, and use all your intelligence to stay one step ahead.

Hiding and Evading

Threat Levels

Soldiers moving into potentially hostile areas must maintain constant awareness of potential and actual threats. In this scenario, the absence of children and women on the street should give cause for concern, as should the figure in the background, watching over the wall. This individual could be a hostile observer, monitoring his enemy's patrol movements in preparation for a possible ambush or kidnap attempt.

capture if his unit is encircled and disarmed. In some instances, pretending to be dead has merit, especially if an enemy is moving quickly and will not hang around to consolidate ground. During the airborne component of the D-Day landings in June 1944, US soldier John Steele of the 505th Parachute Infantry Regiment snagged his parachute on the church tower in the centre of Sainte-Mère-Église, France. Even though the town was bustling with Germans, Steele hung there silently, as if dead, and did so until the Germans pulled out the next day and the town fell into American hands. Such an approach has its risks. If an enemy soldier has an inkling that someone is feigning death, he is more likely to put a bullet or bayonet into the body than inspect closely. For these reasons, it is often far better to find a good hiding place (see below for recommendations), and wait until nightfall to move and cross friendly lines.

Basic Precautions

In the context of modern counter-insurgency warfare, more personal threats to liberty have arisen. Terrorist factions and insurgent groups can extract dark publicity from the capture of just one enemy soldier. On Sunday 25 June 2006, Corporal Gilad Shalit of the Armor Corps, Israel Defence Forces (IDF), was kidnapped by members of the Palestinian

British Army Tip: Kidnapping

For small military units conducting patrols, manning checkpoints or outposts, mounting raids and performing general peacekeeping, there are common ingredients in many kidnap situations:

- Small units become lost within urban or remote rural areas, primarily through navigational errors or having to follow detours because of unexpected obstructions or troublesome terrain.
- Soldiers manning outposts or checkpoints are too few in number to make a convincing defence, and are often isolated from reinforcements.
- Units have to travel regularly along particularly dangerous routes, in areas where the rule of law is weak and insurgent groups dominate the local population.
- Kidnappings can sometimes involve local people known to the prisoners; certain individuals can feign friendship, while at the same time leading soldiers into compromising situations.
- Getting caught in an ambush – many kidnappings happen opportunistically, when a soldier or small unit is isolated during an ambush or improvised explosive device (IED) attack.
- A vehicle is disabled, either through an ambush or because of mechanical failure, leaving those aboard stranded in a single, vulnerable location while they wait for assistance.
- Special forces soldiers, through their common repurposing as VIP bodyguards, are all too aware of these factors, and so have developed a rigorous set of tactical behaviours that dramatically lessen the chances of being kidnapped in the first place. We will look at some of these rules in this chapter, before turning to explore in detail the fundamental techniques of evasion on the ground.

militant organization Hamas, following a raid on an Israeli outpost in the southern Gaza Strip. (Two other IDF soldiers were killed, and three wounded.) At the time of writing (2011), Shalit was still in captivity, his vulnerable position used as a political bargaining chip in the troubled region.

With the ongoing deployments of Western forces in Afghanistan and Iraq, kidnap awareness training has become critical, albeit erratically

Varied Routes

For military units moving regularly between fixed destinations in hostile territory, it is imperative to vary the journey regularly and inventively, to prevent the enemy identifying a predictable route along which they can set up an ambush.

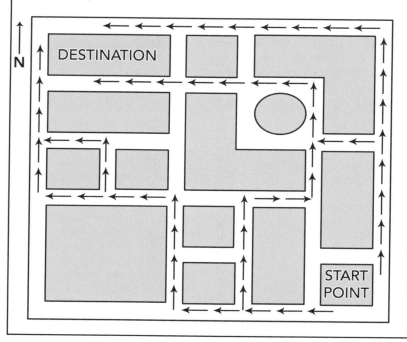

Iraq Kidnapping, 2007

On 29 May 2007 in Baghdad, at 11:50 (local time), five British nationals were kidnapped by Iraqi militants in Baghdad. The kidnapping was not the first in the country since the invasion of 2003, but its circumstances set alarm bells ringing amongst the security community. The incident did not occur on an isolated rural road or in an enemy-held urban zone, but in the Finance Ministry building in east Baghdad. Nor were the victims all amateurs – four of them were ex-military working as bodyguards and security personnel (the other man was a local IT consultant). Eyewitness accounts revealed that the militants arrived in force – possibly up to 100 men – most dressed in police and military uniforms and carrying authentic documentation (they were led by what appeared to be a police major). They entered the building, bursting into a lecture room and shouting 'Where are the foreigners?' Once a group of Westerners were identified, they were overwhelmed, bundled into a van and taken away for a long period of captivity. The four security guards were eventually executed, while the IT consultant was freed. A sixth man, another IT consultant, avoided kidnapping by hiding under floorboards during the initial attack.

distributed. Such training focuses on key techniques and tactical policies to reduce the chances of being taken prisoner.

Vary your route, vary your times

Insurgents and terrorist groups thrive on predictability. If, for example, they know that a military supply convoy travels along a main road between two cities every weekday morning at 08:30–09:30, they are able to plan and coordinate the most efficient attack possible, based on days of observational intelligence.

For this reason, in contested areas foot patrols or vehicular units have to vary their routes of travel on a daily basis, to avoid forming any regular patterns of movement of which the enemy can take advantage. Times of travel must also change regularly – military bases are often under enemy watch, and insurgents can report predictable times of departure to ambush or pursuit groups. Good knowledge of local threat areas is critical in all defensive route planning. Except on offensive operations, or if there is literally no choice, any route should avoid areas of particular danger – ie, those that have known heavy concentrations of enemy forces. If a high-threat route must be taken, a unit needs to make sure that it has the offensive firepower to handle itself in an attack.

Know your route

Getting lost is one of the most dangerous situations for a small unit in insurgent-dominated territory. Preparation is the key to preventing this situation. Each member of the patrol, especially the team leaders (officers and NCOs), should have a

GPS Guidance

Hand-held and vehicle-mounted GPS devices are excellent navigational tools, but they are not failsafe, and should always be used alongside conventional methods of navigation.

Special Forces Tip: Move Carefully, Keep Moving

Ambushes and kidnapping attempts tend to be launched in predictable locations. These include:

- Places where a road narrows between natural or urban features.
- Around sharp bends (the bend limits visibility around the corner, where a roadblock or improvised obstacle could be set up).
- Isolated outposts.
- Footpaths and trails that channel a patrol along a predictable route.
- Difficult terrain, such as mountains or woodland, which can disperse a patrol.
- Any urban zone, which provides insurgents with familiar attack

and escape routes, and which limits vehicular manoeuvres in response.
• Bridges, fords and any other controlled crossing points.

In hostile areas, streets such as these should be avoided at all costs. The vehicles act as rough roadblocks, channelling patrols into ambush zones.

sound grasp of the overall area of operations (AO), including all its major and minor roads, bridges, rivers and streams, and centres of habitation. The soldiers should also be able to identify several landmarks against which they can orient themselves if lost. If, for example, they know that a particular river runs on an east–west orientation, this can form a general guide to their axis of patrol. Similarly, understanding sun navigation (see Chapter 6, page 276) will provide a celestial hint when a wrong turn has been taken. Most importantly, vehicular units should not depend solely satellite navigation systems: Global Positioning System (GPS) information should not be given priority over good maps and prior knowledge.

The common thread running through this list is that ambushes often occur where a unit has to follow a fixed route of travel through a confined or dispersing space, with limited options for manoeuvring out of trouble should the worst occur. Ambush sites also work by slowing the movement of the unit as it passes into the 'kill zone'.

Sensible precautions can help to mitigate the threat somewhat (although in active insurgency wars it can never be removed entirely). When approaching sharp bends in a vehicle or on foot, slow down and swing out wide to give yourself a direct line of observation around the corner before turning. Check your surroundings carefully. Are there any individuals or groups watching your movements from a distance? Are they talking into a mobile phone, or filming with a video camera? These could be innocent actions; conversely, the individual could be acting as a coordinating observer for an ambush, relaying instructions about your

Avoiding an Ambush

A professional ambush will hit a military column at several points simultaneously, destroying lead and rear vehicles and trapping forces between these points. Units should try to avoid narrow routes flanked on both sides by high ground.

movements to the main attack group. Does a road or track seem to be littered with strategically placed obstacles, as if channelling your direction of travel to a certain point?

In an urban zone or village, does everything seem suspiciously quiet? Insurgents will often inform local people to keep off the streets when an attack is planned, and well-trained soldiers note that an absence of children is particularly concerning.

Typical responses to such ominous signs are:

- Increased vigilance – scan your eyes constantly across your surroundings, looking carefully at windows, street corners, the roofs of buildings, ditches, areas of vegetation and anywhere else figures could be hiding or waiting.
- Preparation – prepare to defend yourself. Weapons should be loaded and ready to fire, presented in the direction of likely threats. Make sure you are wearing any available body army and your helmet, and that your comrades are doing likewise.
- Find another route – take a different route, as long as you know exactly where you are going and the new direction doesn't increase the threat levels. Choose routes that give you good open fields of fire and plenty of escape options.
- Keep moving – a moving target is much harder to shoot at than a static one. Keep moving at a steady pace through the danger area, and if an ambush is sprung accelerate as fast as possible out

of the 'kill zone' while applying heavy suppressive firepower.

Know your friends

As the feature on page 18 above indicates, kidnappers can cloak themselves in the appearance of official personnel, or even friends. At some point, local people have to be trusted to build 'hearts and minds' relationships, and a soldier must never fall into the alienating trap of thinking everyone is a suspect. There are, however, some precautions a soldier can take when working with unknown personnel.

First, try to make sure that everyone is properly vetted. This means looking into his or her personal and family background to check for any previous connections with known insurgency groups or leaders. Try to find out if he has significant financial concerns – insurgent recruiters find that the offer of money is a simple and effective recruiting tool. Be cautious if very little information is available; does this mean that he has been recruited from outside the area?

Second, observe his behaviour on a daily basis. Does he exhibit flashes of hostility, or ask frequent and unwarranted questions about your whereabouts or future plans? Have you ever seen him taking photographs (either on a camera or a mobile phone) of key military installations and hardware, or

disappearing at strange moments to talk on his phone? Such behaviours can have legitimate explanations, but they might also put you on alert, and prompt you for further intelligence on the individual, or even his redeployment away from sensitive areas of operations.

Also be very alert if you see unusually large gatherings of people, for which there isn't a ready explanation. Many soldiers have been

All-round Awareness

For soldiers, team-work is a true lifesaver. Here this US vehicle-mounted patrol fans out around the Stryker, with each member of the team exercising responsibility for watching over over a particular sector, the combined sectors adding up to a vigilance of 360°.

kidnapped during episodes of social unrest, such as riots, particularly when they become separated from colleagues. Finally, make sure that everyone can present correct paperwork. Even if the document appears genuine and correct – which it might well be – occasionally do spot background checks on the holder via intelligence units to see if they throw up any anomalies against databases or other records.

Secure your surroundings

Many kidnappings take place from military outposts and checkpoints, or from public buildings where soldiers and other key personnel congregate. (Rarely will insurgent groups attack major military bases, apart from with stand-off means such as rockets and mortars.) Whatever your location, always maintain awareness and vigilance. Note the entrances and exits of all rooms you enter, and try

Tip: Spotting Improvised Explosive Devices (IEDs)

In both conventional and unconventional warfare, ambushes are often initiated explosively. IEDs in particular have become the scourge of armies in war zones such as Vietnam, Iraq and Afghanistan – in Iraq between 2003 and 2010, IEDs accounted for 70 per cent of all US casualties. Spotting them is no mean feat, as both device and deployment have reached high levels of sophistication. The following, however, are some typical containers/locations/signs of emplaced IEDs:

- Human or animal remains in strange or prominent locations.
- Damaged vehicles placed by the sides of roads.
- Displaced kerbstones or pavement slabs, or unattended boxes.

- Strangely positioned piles of earth, wood or refuse.
- Disturbed ground or vegetation.
- Indications of road repair, such as freshly filled-in potholes where official work hasn't been taking place.
- Walls showing signs of modification, such as new brickwork or plastering, in otherwise dilapidated areas.
- Wires or cables snaking into the ground, perhaps leading to a building.

If an IED is suspected, the area should be avoided – ideally put several hundred metres between you and the potential blast zone. Stay behind cover – and call in the bomb-disposal experts.

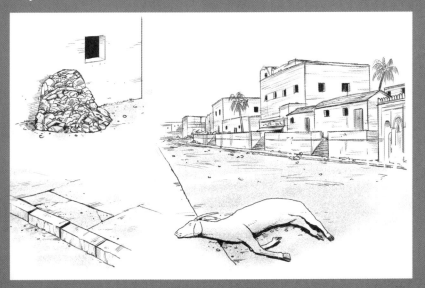

to avoid cornering yourself in a location from which there would be no escape. In high-risk areas, secure doors and windows properly, to prevent easy access, and ensure that all surveillance and alarm systems are functioning, with no 'blind spots' around the building.

Outposts or checkpoints should be configured to provide 360-degree observation, and have open fields of fire all round. Approach roads must be secured with staggered obstacles or other barriers to prevent fast vehicular approach, and everyone manning the position has to be clear about the rules of engagement (RoE). There must be an understandable system of warnings (such as an audible warning followed by a smoke grenade) before opening fire with live ammunition.

Be prepared to fight

The precautions above can limit, but not remove, your chances of being taken prisoner. The fact remains that in a war zone danger is generally unavoidable. Based on recent experiences in Iraq and Afghanistan, the need to stay out of the kidnappers' hands is paramount, so if a unit is ambushed or attacked, then it must fight back – and hard. The standard response to attack is to find cover and return instant and heavy suppressive firepower. Kidnappers will need to get close to take someone captive, and if the price for doing so becomes too high, there is a strong likelihood that they will back off, or at least be pinned down while you call in reinforcements. Target any hostile individuals who seem to be giving orders, or who wear officer rank, to 'behead' the attackers' command. Also watch out for spectators high up on buildings, particularly if they are talking into mobile phones – they could be providing real-time intelligence to the enemy. Warn them in no uncertain terms to move away or risk being shot. All firefights can have uncertain outcomes, but the harder the response to an attack, the less chance you have of being taken.

Deciding to Move

One of the most dangerous situations a warrior can face is being separated from his unit behind enemy lines, or in enemy-dominated territory. The circumstances through which this can happen vary enormously. An airman might be shot down over a hostile state; a marine could be separated from his squad in the confusion of battle; a vehicle might be disabled by an IED, leaving its occupants stranded. Regardless of the situation, however, it is a near certainty that the unless the soldier is apprehended immediately, he or she is going to have to rely on evasion techniques to stay out of captivity.

A first response, if friendly forces aren't within easy reach, is to find a

Using Natural Terrain

Soldiers conducting evasion should use every scrap of cover they can find. Look for terrain that will stand directly between you and a line-of-sight observer.

secure hiding place. 'Secure' is the keyword. Following a major battle, enemy troops will be all too aware that isolated soldiers might be scattered and hiding, and will search accordingly. For this reason, obvious hiding places such as farm outbuildings or huts are to be discouraged, unless those locations have decent hiding places within them. Be careful about secreting yourself in places surrounded by animals or livestock. With their acute senses, animals might become interested in a sweaty, anxious soldier hunkered down in their midst, and their behaviour is likely to draw the attention of enemy search parties.

When choosing a good hiding place, remember that anywhere you are reluctant to go, the enemy will also probably be reluctant to look. Your 'hole-up site' (to use US military speak) can therefore be places such

Seaman Dale E. Land

On 15 November 1942, the destroyer USS *Walke* was sunk by Japanese naval attack off the island of Guadalcanal in the Pacific. One of the survivors was Seaman Dale E. Land, who along with machinist's mate Harold Taylor floated for some two days in the sea before being washed ashore on the island near Tassafaronga. American lines lay to the east, but to get there the men had to pass through dense jungle teeming with Japanese forces. Dead Japanese soldiers provided them with a rifle and some ammunition, and they set off for safety. The journey was arduous in the extreme. The two men survived on coconuts and a few biscuits taken from the Japanese bodies, and for safety they could travel only at night. The landscape was a mixture of near-impenetrable foliage and sucking swamps, and both men were severely bitten by the local insect life. They were involved in several small-scale firefights with local Japanese units, during one of which Taylor was shot and killed. Now on his own, Land kept going towards friendly lines, evading the enemy search party that was now on his trail and attempting to cope with the high fever from which he was suffering. Eventually, on 5 December, he found US troops of the 182nd Regiment, and fell into safe hands. His evasion had lasted three weeks through some of the most hostile terrain in the Pacific.

as drainage culverts, large waste pipes, areas of heavily overgrown terrain, inaccessible attics or basements, abandoned factories – anywhere where you are securely hidden from view. You should ideally find a hiding place near to your last-known position, as it will be there

that friendly search-and-rescue parties will begin their hunt for you. Yet the reality of conditions on the ground might dictate that you have to move.

Staying with your vehicle/aircraft (if that is your situation) is the preferred option in most cases. Even if you don't

Dog Evasion

Tracker dogs work best when following a single, unbroken line of scent. By winding your route around obstacles and by crossing water, you can either make the dog turn back on itself, or lose your track entirely.

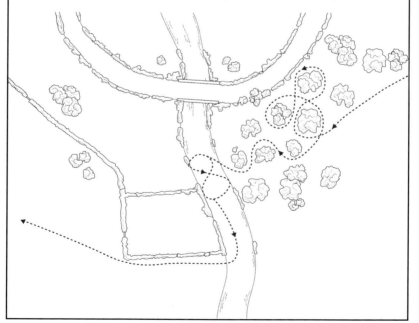

US Army Tip: Stay or Go?

A US multi-service manual published in 1999, entitled *Survival, Evasion, and Recovery*, issued the following advice for knowing when to move and when to stay where you are:

1. STAY OR MOVE CONSIDERATIONS
a. Stay with the vehicle/aircraft in a non-combat environment.
b. Leave only when –
   (1) Dictated by the threat.
   (2) Are certain of your location, have a known destination, and have the ability to get there.
   (3) Can reach water, food, shelter, and/or help.
   (4) Convinced rescue is not coming.
c. Consider the following if you decide to travel:
   (1) Follow the briefed evasion plan.
   (2) Determine which direction to travel and why.
   (3) Decide what equipment to take, cache, or destroy.

have working radio systems with you (see Chapter 6 for more about survival communications), the locating tools for modern military forces are highly sophisticated, including aerial reconnaissance and satellite surveillance. Moreover, some vehicles/aircraft will be fitted with transponders, such as the Grenadier Beyond Line of Sight Reporting And Tracking (BRAT) system. If fitted or carried (they can be small enough to drop into a backpack), these provide automatic, real-time location data back to a headquarters station via the GPS network. This information can then be used to vector rescue forces directly to your location. Such is a far safer option than wandering uncertainly around enemy territory.

Yet circumstances might transpire that moving away from your last-known location becomes imperative. In many war zones, and particularly in urban insurgency contexts, crippled vehicles or downed aircraft are a magnet for enemy forces, and with every minute that passes the human volume of threat can increase. Furthermore, members of special forces units may be conducting missions in which they know that help

Movement and Tracking

Remember that trackers are looking for evidence of your passing, such as those given below. Two or three pieces of 'sign', mentally connected together, will give the enemy your direction of movement, so try to disturb the environment as little as possible.

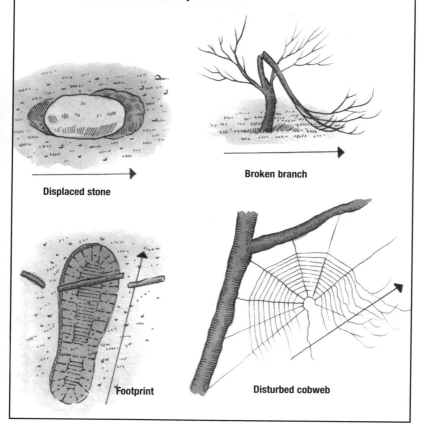

Displaced stone

Broken branch

Footprint

Disturbed cobweb

will not be coming any time soon, especially if their operation is of a sensitive nature in a foreign country. In those cases, if a mission goes wrong the soldiers will usually follow a pre-agreed escape plan, such as moving themselves to a more convenient border area for extraction. The key point, as explained in the box on page 32, is that if you do decide to move you do so *purposefully,* with a definite objective and a known destination. While on the move, however, the most important consideration now becomes staying out of sight.

Know Your Enemy

Evasion in a high-threat environment is mentally and physically challenging to the highest degree. Not only do you have to cope with the sheer physical demands of staying alive in the wilderness (if that is where your evasion takes place), but you also have to pit your intelligence and skills in evasion against the tracking efforts of the enemy.

An enemy who is looking for you with determination will have a range of resources at his disposal, varying in their degree of sophistication.

Search party

Search parties (also known as 'tracking teams') are the most time-tested method of hunting down soldiers on the run. The threat they pose depends much on their composition. They might be a few

ill-trained and resentful soldiers rummaging around the bush without purpose, or they could be highly trained special forces tracking units with sophisticated tools at their disposal. The greater the size of the search party, the more eyes it can bring to bear on the terrain, but the slower it moves compared to a small team. Professional search parties will therefore often consist of a relatively small group of personnel, which include a team leader, assistant leader and security men. The team leader will generally be an expert in tracking, although the team might also include local civilian individuals who know the terrain well and understand where you might be hiding or moving towards.

Search parties tend to operate in methodical ways. They will begin the search at your last-known location, where they will attempt to pick up visible signs of your direction of movement. The trackers will then either following the trail of 'sign' or 'displacement' or search out from the last-known position in a methodical pattern. As a general principle, a human engaged in search activities will scan the ground in front of him to a distance of 10–15m (32–49ft) and in an arc of 180° to his front – this can be useful knowledge if you want to stay just out of range of eyeline.

Typically, the team leader will make a judgement about your possible routes of travel, based on the fact that you want either to travel directly to friendly lines or forces; or to get to a suitable position for an extraction.

Tracker dogs

Tracker dogs are an age-old threat to the soldier on evasion. Trained to pick up and track strange scents undetectable to human noses, they dramatically improve the accuracy and tracking speed of the search party (a good tracker dog can follow a trail at a speed of up to 16km/h /10mph). Although a dog's vision is

Hiding Place

This culvert could provide an ideal escape route from enemy search parties. Following it through could lead to a secure egress point in the dense wooded area beyond, while the water will make job of the tracker dog much harder in terms of following your scent.

Search Techniques

This basic search technique is known as the 'square search'. Essentially the search party starts at your last-known position and then searches outwards in an ever-expanding pattern of 'squares', with right-angled turns at regular intervals.

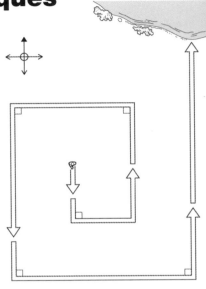

not superior to that of a human, its sense of smell is roughly 900 times better than that of a human, and its hearing is 40 times greater.

When tracking by scent, the dog works by obtaining a 'scent picture' of the fugitive, an olfactory profile based on sweat scent deposited on the ground or surrounding objects or on other odours such as personal hygiene products. One reason never to drop personal items while on the run is that a dog-handler team can use them to give the dog a

'reinforcing scent', a model of your particular smell that improves the tracking.

The efficiency of a tracking dog is not limitless, and their ability to follow a scent is affected by a variety of environmental factors. For best tracking results, the dog must obtain a fresh scent at a verified starting point (typically your last-known position). The ideal weather conditions for dog tracking are night-time and early morning, and cool, cloudy weather with little wind –

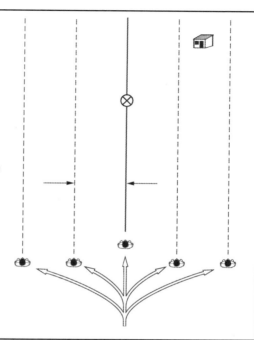

Here the search party adopts a different configuration, moving in one direction with each member of the team a fixed distance apart. This system will move quickly in one direction, and relies on a good central tracker to coordinate the team's movement.

these conditions limit the evaporation or dispersal of sweat particles. Thick vegetation is also conducive tracking terrain – the sweat clings to the foliage and isn't dispersed easily. Conversely, the dog's nose power is limited by hot, dry conditions (in which sweat evaporates quickly), or on days of strong winds and heavy rain, both of which degrade the scent signature. Dogs can also struggle to follow your scent accurately across water, snow and shifting sands, or if your scent

trail traverses an area with many other competing smells, such as urban terrain or fertilized fields.

Helicopters
A helicopter is the ultimate search device, capable of covering hundreds of miles of territory at great speed. Although it is actually relatively easy to hide from a helicopter when you hear it coming, if the terrain allows, the common use of forward-looking infrared (FLIR) cameras means that the helicopter crew can search large

Helicopter Search

A classic search pattern adopted by a helicopter crew is to start from the evader's last-known position, then fly outwards in a series of ever-increasing circles. Technologies such as forward-looking infrared (FLIR) cameras ensure that the search helicopter is one of an evader's most dangerous opponents.

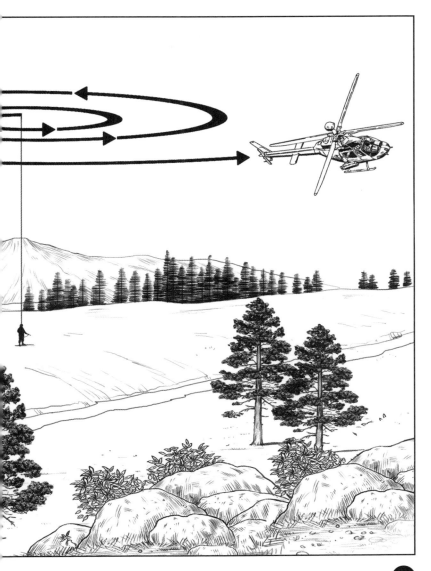

areas with thermal imaging, and from high-up vantage points. Helicopters can also spoil your extraction plans by regularly patrolling suspected rescue areas. Their crew can also stay in direct radio contact with ground-based search parties; between them, they form a visual and technological net from which it can be hard to escape.

Technological resources
A tracking team will have all the usual optical search devices at its disposal, such as binoculars and the telescopic sights on rifles. Obviously these devices have limited applications at night (the period of the day when you are most likely to be moving), but remember that during these hours the team might well have night-vision technologies (NVTs) to fall back on. Three types of NVT are available:

- Image intensification – collects and magnifies available light (such as moonlight and starlight) through an optical lens.
- Active illumination – an image-intensifying technology combined with an infrared illumination source.
- Thermal imaging – a camera that creates an image by distinguishing heat contrasts in the environment.

Active illumination and thermal imaging present the gravest threats

to the evader at night. The latter in particular is especially powerful because it can 'see' your body heat through certain objects, such as foliage, even though you might be hidden from sight. (For this reason, thermal imaging can also be used during daylight hours as a search device.) Your only protection is to position yourself behind or within something that blocks your heat emissions entirely from view, such as in a cave or building. Alternatively, you could act as if you are a local civilian going about his daily business; the thermal image portrays only your heat contours, not accurate visual details, so the device operator might assume you are nobody suspicious.

Out of Sight
Unlike in a civilian survival situation, where you actually want to increase your visibility and be found, in a evasion situation your overarching goal is to stay hidden. For this purpose, the fundamentals of camouflage and concealment come into play.

Although the mnemonics for the principles of camouflage and concealment vary between services and nations, the following 'Seven S's' cover all the key bases. They are:

- Shape.
- Shine.
- Silhouette.

Blending In

In a wilderness setting, you need to make every aspect of your body and equipment blend in with the surroundings. Avoid straight lines – this arctic-warfare sniper has dispersed the line of his rifle barrel with a draped cloth.

Helmet Camouflage

By attaching vegetation to his helmet, this soldier breaks up his head silhouette. The key to such camouflage is to keep it fresh and to ensure that it matches precisely the terrain through which you are moving.

- Shadow.
- Sound.
- Speed.
- Surroundings.

Shape

'Shape' refers to the contours of the human body. In a wilderness environment, these contours stand out easily. Your objective is not to render yourself invisible – which is, of course, impossible – but to disperse your shape visually so that it is difficult to spot against the background of the landscape.

A terrain-specific camouflage uniform does much of the hard work reducing your visual profile, but don't rely on it exclusively. There are improvisational methods of improving your camouflage. Attach *local* vegetation to key parts of your body and your dress – such as your helmet, shoulders and any parts of the body that form a 'V' (armpits and crotch); don't overdo this, as a large walking bush will attract more attention than an unadorned person. Make sure that the vegetation matches the surroundings, and be prepared to change it when moving into different terrain. Also refresh the vegetation regularly – once it starts to die, it will change colour, and stand out against the background.

Another method of camouflage is to create an improvised 'ghillie suit'. Attach short strips of naturally coloured material all over your

uniform, thereby fragmenting your outline. Such suits are often worn by snipers and special forces soldiers on concealed deployments, but the options for making one are admittedly likely to be limited if you are on the run. Help from sympathetic locals might make this possible, however.

Shine

Shine refers to anything that might either reflect light or transmit light, and hence give your position away to keen eyes. Skin, for example, can be highly reflective, especially if bathed in sweat or if oily. You should therefore camouflage and mute all bare skin with greasepaint or an improvised substance (charcoal, boot polish, mud, crushed berries, etc), focusing on the areas of prominent shine such as nose, cheekbones, chin, ears and forehead. Apply the same to hands, or wear dark gloves. As with camouflage, vary the pattern according to the local terrain. 'Blotch' patterns tend to suit temperate deciduous, desert and snowy regions, while 'slash' patterns are ideal for coniferous woodland, jungles and grasslands (see illustrations pages 44–45). The two can be used together for mixed terrain, but again, show restraint – any overuse of camouflage can actually increase your visibility.

Other sources of shine include your equipment and any personal

Face Camouflage

The 'blotch' pattern of face camouflage here is ideally suited to temperate deciduous (leaf-shedding) areas, desert and barren, snowy landscapes. Don't overdo the dark areas – too much dark camouflage can make you stand out even more.

The 'slash' pattern of camouflage is designed for coniferous, jungle and grassy areas, the long, contrasting stripes down the face blending in with the vertical lines of the surrounding vegetation.

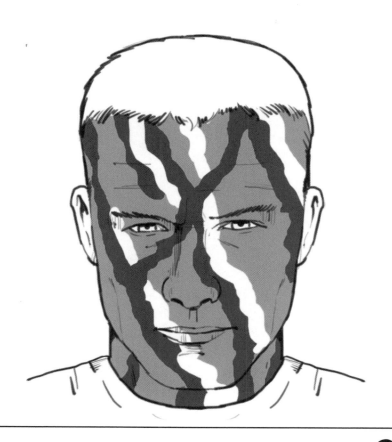

US Army Tip: Critical Factors in Evasion Success

1. Planning.
   b. Guidelines for successful evasion include –
      (1) Keeping a positive attitude.
      (2) Using established procedures.
      (3) Following your evasion plan of action.
      (4) Being patient.
      (5) Drinking water (DO NOT eat food without water).
      (6) Conserving strength for critical periods.
      (7) Resting and sleeping as much as possible.
      (8) Staying out of sight.
   c. The following odors stand out and may give an evader away:
      (1) Scented soaps and shampoos.
      (2) Shaving cream, after-shave lotion, or other cosmetics.
      (3) Insect repellent (camouflage stick is least scented).
      (4) Gum and candy (smell is strong or sweet).
      (5) Tobacco (odor is unmistakable).
   d. Where to go (initiate evasion plan of action):
      (1) Near a suitable area for recovery.
      (2) Selected area for evasion.
      (3) Neutral or friendly country or area.
      (4) Designated area for recovery.

– *Survival, Evasion, and Recovery: Multiservice Procedures For Survival, Evasion, And Recovery* (Air Land Sea Application Center, 1999)

belongings. Dull any shiny metal objects, such as weapon receivers, with paint, mud, boot polish, candle smoke or whatever is to hand. (Be careful with a piece of equipment so that you do not affect its important functions.) Alternatively, cover any reflective surfaces with ghillie strips or fabric mesh. Pay particular attention to camouflaging optical lenses (binoculars, sights, etc) – if the sunlight catches these, the

Using Concealment

Dense vegetation is ideal for providing concealment from view. Be aware, however, that concealment is not the same as cover – vegetation will provide no protection from small-arms fire.

resulting flash can be seen many miles away. Also be careful if you are carrying a mobile phone with you. Shield it completely from external eyes if you have to use it – think how much a mobile screen stands out if someone uses his phone in a darkened cinema. The same applies to any other artificial light sources, such as torches or keyring lights. Above all, *do not* smoke, under any circumstances: the brief pleasure of a cigarette can betray you via both its light and smell.

Silhouette

Few things stand out more prominently than a person silhouetted on the brow of a hill, or against a strong artificial light. The best conceivable camouflage is useless in such situations, so it is vital that you avoid breaking the skyline and make sure you use 'dead ground' constantly. 'Dead ground' consists of areas of terrain in which you are shielded from external eyes, such as the bottom of a deep ditch or behind thick vegetation. If necessary, adopt

Evasion in Yugoslavia

On 2 June 1995, Scott O'Grady, a USAF F-16C pilot, was shot down by an SA-6 'Gainful' missile while flying as part of Operation *Deny Flight* over Bosnia and Herzegovina, in the former Yugoslavia. He managed to eject safely, but was deposited deep behind enemy lines, with Serbian forces actively hunting for him. As he landed, he shed his parachute and immediately covered his face with mud as camouflage, while also putting on green gloves to shield his hands. He went into cover in deep foliage, and on occasions the Serbian search parties literally stood a few feet from him, without discovering his whereabouts. Each night O'Grady would shift his location to better cover, staying within 3.2km (2 miles) of his last-known position. He survived for six days in this manner, living off the contents of his survival pack plus leaves, grass and some insects. His most important piece of kit was his PRC-112 survival radio, via which he managed to establish contact with US forces. A massive air rescue operation was mounted, and on the morning of 8 June he was plucked to safety by a Sea Stallion helicopter, despite Serbian forces opening fire on the rescuers.

Parallel Crossing

When crossing horizontal features such as fences, keep the body parallel to the ground at all times, to reduce your silhouette to a viewer in the distance. Throw bulky equipment over first before crossing.

Horizon Silhouette

When moving through a landscape, avoid silhouetting your body on the horizon. The soldier here has stopped on the crest of a hill, making himself stand out against the sky and presenting an ideal target for an enemy sniper or rifleman.

Light Silhouette

Strong light sources create silhouette and shadow, both of which can betray your presence. Remember that the lower the light source to the horizon or the floor, the longer the shadow on the floor.

a crawling position to keep yourself out of sight. Remember also that darkness does not protect you from the dangers of silhouetting; a moonlit night sky is perfectly bright enough to carve your outline in stark relief if you stray from the dead ground. Also be very aware of any artificial light sources, such as vehicle headlights or floodlights. If you are between them and an observer, you can be shown up in sharp, dark contrast to the light. Always keep a literally low profile; if you have to cross a feature such as a fence, either go under it or roll your body across the top, keeping parallel to the structure.

Shadow

Shadows are both your friend and enemy in an evasion situation. On the positive side, you can use shadows to reduce your silhouette and shine. For example, if you have to cross a sun-washed road, you can use the shadow of a large tree falling across the road as a safer path to the other side. Negatively, shadows can expand your visible 'footprint' significantly. A low bright sun can, if you are standing up, project a dark black shadow many metres long across the floor, making you more conspicuous to both ground observers and to those in the air. Travelling only at night is the obvious way to avoid sun shadow (although shadows from artificial lights remain an issue), but as a general principle

always be aware of both the direction and length of your shadow, and use dead ground to minimize your exposure to direct light.

Sound

Noise discipline is just as important as visual discipline during an evasion. In perfect conditions – still, crisp nights in flat terrain (especially deserts) – the chink of a belt buckle on a rifle could be heard hundreds of

Using Shadow

When crossing a road, the shadows thrown by trees can create good routes to cross from one side to another. Stay low and move fast, and try to keep noise to a minimum.

metres away. Louder noises, such as a gunshot, can resound for miles.

A first test of noise discipline is to jump up and down on the spot (only if it is safe to do so, obviously). If you note that anything rattles or knocks, try to stick it down with tape or tie it down with a strip of material. (Don't do anything to your weapon that will impair the free movement of the bolt or the processes of ejection or reloading.) Make sure that all straps on your equipment are tightened properly, as ill-fitted equipment is far more likely to make a noise. Turn off any electronic equipment with alarms, regular chimes or other effects.

A major source of noise when you are trying to be secretive is your actual footsteps. In natural environments, and while moving at night, you constantly run the risk of stepping on a twig, which then breaks

and gives off an unhelpful locating 'crack'. Special forces soldiers use distinctive steps to lessen this possibility. When stepping forwards, raise your knee high and lower the toe carefully to the floor, brushing aside vegetation before gently planting the heel. Alternatively, lower your heel first and make a sweeping action with your toes to clear a space into which you put your weight. When moving through foliage, avoid the temptation to grab and snap off awkward branches. Such will not only give an audible signal, but the white, broken end of the branch will later indicate that someone has passed through. Note that the weather can help you out with noise discipline. If you travel on a windy, rainy night, the drumming, rushing weather will mostly mask the sounds of your

Staying Low

When moving through high-risk areas with the enemy nearby, adopt a low crawl, working your way forwards using your elbows and knees. If behind vegetation, maintain observation by looking *through* the leaves and branches, not at them.

travel, and has the added benefit of forcing many enemy troops to seek shelter rather than pursue you.

Speed

'Speed' in the evasion context is essentially an alternative term for 'movement'. It can be taken literally, however. In high-risk areas with a heavy enemy presence, reduce the speed of your movements to a

careful and considered pace. Make sure that you have a plan before you leave a safe position – set yourself a destination, and be generous in the time allowed to get there. Choose a viable route that offers you plenty of cover and concealment. (More about route planning is explored in Chapter 6.) Move through the landscape at a steady pace, quick enough to make progress but not so fast that you become exhausted and then careless. Take regular short breaks, not only to recuperate but also so that you may check for signs of any enemy pursuit or activity. Make every action deliberate and considered, thinking about noise and light discipline constantly. Remember that it takes only one lapse to give your position away.

Surroundings

A search party studies the landscape in the hope of spotting anything unusual or unnatural, which could indicate either your direct presence or that you have passed through recently. For this reason, try to leave as few actual signs of your presence on the surroundings as possible. Don't break twigs or flatten grasses; instead, push them aside with a stick, move through, and then let them move naturally back into position. Watch where you put your feet. Moving across hard ground leaves relatively few examples of 'sign' (indicators of your presence), whereas walking through mud will often leave

Betraying your Presence

The illustrations here show ways in which you can give your position away to enemy searchers. An evader has to be aware of sound, light and smell in all their forms, and also of leaving any evidence of his presence behind in the wilderness, such as litter or footprints.

deep and clear footprint impressions. (Be especially careful if walking from mud onto rocky ground, as the resulting muddy footprints on the rock will stand out with comic-book clarity.) Don't overturn logs or large rocks, and if you have built a shelter try to disperse the pieces before leaving it. Should you spot an animal such as a bird or deer, try to allow it to move away naturally rather than startle it – startled animals are a good sign to

US Armed Forces Tip

Mask unavoidable tracks in soft footing by:

(a) Placing tracks in the shadows of vegetation, downed logs, and snowdrifts.
(b) Moving before and during precipitation allows tracks to fill in.
(c) Traveling during windy periods.
(d) Taking advantage of solid surfaces (logs, rocks, etc.) leaving less evidence of travel.
(e) Patting out tracks lightly to speed their breakdown or make them look old.

– *Survival, Evasion, and Recovery* (1999)

enemy search parties looking for signs of your passing.

Discipline

You must be very disciplined about not dropping litter or leaving behind items of equipment, as these will be the clearest pieces of sign to your pursuers. If you have to defecate, either do so in a bag and take it with you, or bury it in an inconspicuous location. In short, your aim is to leave

Dangerous Crossing

As with the description of crossing fences on page 49, moving across rail lines requires that you stay low and parallel to the floor. Move quickly, however, and ensure that you cross to a position of concealment on the other side of the tracks.

your surroundings exactly as you found them.

Staying Ahead

Implementing all the above disciplines will in themselves make life especially difficult for your pursuers. There are other measures,

however, that can help you stay out of their hands, if intelligently applied.

Official US military advice states that at 'irregular intervals' you should:

(a) STOP at a point of concealment.
(b) LOOK for signs of human or animal activity (smoke, tracks,

aircraft, weapons, animals, etc.
(d) SMELL for vehicles, troops,
  animals, fires, etc.

This sound advice includes a point about the nature of peripheral vision at night or in low-light conditions. If you spot a suspicious silhouette at night, staring straight at it will result only in its visual disappearance into a granular dark mass. Instead, move your eyes around the sides and edges of the object, and use your peripheral vision to provide identification.

As has been indicated above, you can use the weather and terrain to your advantage when evading pursuers. Poor weather, particularly a combination of rain and strong winds, will provide a high degree of ambient cover and concealment. If conditions are severe enough, they can even ground search aircraft, or simply reduce their effectiveness via a low cloud base. A search helicopter or fixed-wing aircraft will be especially reluctant to fly into hilly, heavily forested, rocky coastal or mountainous areas during periods of bad weather.

roads, troops, vehicles, aircraft, wire, buildings, etc.). Watch for trip wires or booby traps and avoid leaving evidence of travel. Peripheral vision is more effective for recognizing movement at night and twilight.
(c) LISTEN for vehicles, troops,

Confusing signals

The ideal pursuit for a search party, particularly one equipped with tracker dogs, is along a clear, linear route. Therefore, try to confuse both dogs and humans as much as possible. At certain points, double back on yourself, or even walk backwards for a certain distance – your footprints, if you leave any, will show a direction of travel contrary to your actual route. Cross water frequently to throw off the dogs' scent tracking, but also use the water crossings as opportunities to make significant changes in direction. Cover your trail constantly. If you are moving across dry, dusty terrain, dragging a leafy tree bough behind you can help to scatter your footprints.

Creating distance

Another simple evasion technique is simply to outdistance your pursuers. Bearing in mind what we said about cautious movement, this approach is suited to areas of extensive wilderness in which enemy presence is marginal. It involves good physical fitness on your part, but basically requires moving faster and for longer than the search party expects.

Many of the searchers will typically be less committed (albeit marginally so) to capturing you than you are to evading capture, so when physical exhaustion sets in they are likely to stop for a break. If they stop for one hour, during which time you keep moving briskly on, you can extend the gap between you for at least 6.4km (4 miles).

Take care with this approach, however. Rushing breathlessly through a landscape will not only deplete your energy, it will also give

Types of Footprints

Being able to read footprints can give you important clues about pursuers or local civilians. These footprints indicate, from top to bottom:

- **someone running (long strides)**

- **someone carrying a heavy load (feet drag between steps)**

- **a person wearing military-style boots**

- **a woman in stilettoes;**

- **someone walking backwards.**

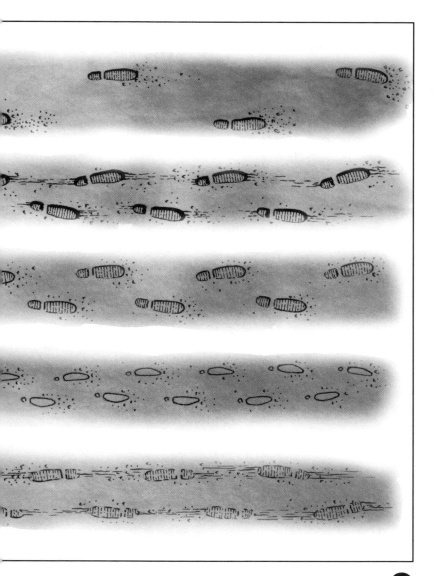

Assessing Foot Traffic

To ascertain how man people have passed a single spot, imagine a box 91cm (36in) square over a series of footprints. Count the number of footprints in the square and then divide by two to give an idea of the number of people who have passed.

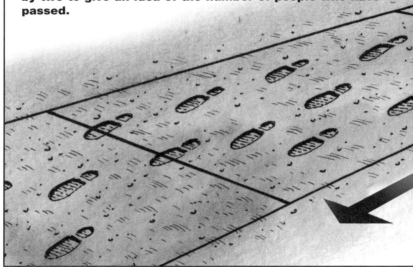

your pursuers a larger volume of tracking information in the form of noise, visual signs (movement attracts attention in a still landscape) and increased sweat output for the tracker dog.

Fighting the trackers

Should the worst happen, and the pursuers appear as if they will be on you imminently, you have several options. First, you could stop and go into hiding, keeping perfectly still and quiet. Hopefully they will actually move past your location, lose the trail further on, and take an erroneous route. Second, you could fight. This option takes both guts and realism, and appropriate weapons. If the search party is small, and you have an automatic firearm or are evading in the

Evasion through Urban Zones

Evasion through hostile urban zones is particularly difficult and fraught with danger. The following tips may be of help:

- Move at night if possible, using more deserted parts of the city (such as wasteland to the sides of major highways) to avoid human traffic.
- Acquire and wear local dress if possible, which at night will act as a form of disguise.
- Before you go on deployment, learn some local greetings and phrases – if someone speaks to you, give a short response and keep moving, as they may just judge you as strange and leave you be.
- Don't wander off into entirely strange neighbourhoods. Use any available communications to get in touch with your unit, then describe to them a prominent landmark so that they can get bearings on your location. Try to find a hiding place and wait for rescue.

company of other soldiers, then an ambush could wipe out the pursuers. If you are on you own and kitted out with nothing more than a pistol, however, then you are advised against it.

More about how to handle direct contact with your pursuers is described in Chapter 5. It may well be that you cannot avoid being caught and captured.

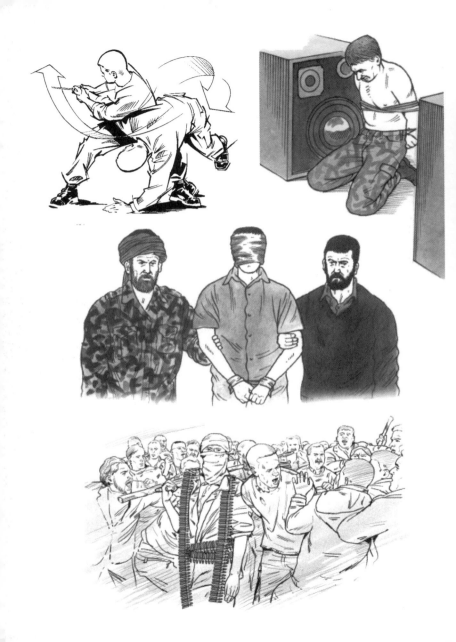

Few experiences in life can be as frightening as being taken prisoner or hostage. Once a captive, a person relinquishes much of the control over his life and future, which both now rest in the hands of his captors. For some, especially those who fall into the hands of professional military personnel with a respect for statutes such as the Geneva Convention, the experience may well be hard but perfectly endurable. For those held by insurgents or more ideologically fanatical enemies, the experience can be the ultimate horror.

While this book is primarily about the skills and tactics required for escape and evasion, we also need to address POW survival. In this uniquely dangerous and mentally exhausting situation, there are well-researched strategies that increase a prisoner's chance of making it through the ordeal, and eventually being rescued.

In the Hands of the Enemy

In October 2002, the Chairman of the Joint Chiefs of Staff, Richard B.

. . . .

A prisoner faces multiple possible challenges – isolation, torture (mental and physical), boredom, fear and life amongst other prisoners. Controlling what can be controlled is vital.

2

Surviving imprisonment or being taken hostage is a hard test of mental stamina and physical resilience, and requires true strength of mind

Capture and Imprisonment

Myers, published the *Antiterrorism Personal Protection Guide: A Self-Help Guide to Terrorism*. The booklet's policy guidance notes explains why it is US prisoners in particular who represent a particular value to an enemy, whether conventional or irregular:

US military personnel captured by terrorists or detained by hostile foreign governments are often held for individual exploitation, to influence the US Government, or both. This exploitation can take many forms, but each form of exploitation is designed to assist the foreign government or the terrorist captors. In the past, terrorists or governments exploited detainees for information and propaganda efforts, including confessions to crimes never committed. This assisted or lent credibility to the detainer. Governments also have been exploited in such situation to make damaging statements about themselves or to force them to appear weak in relation to other governments. Governments have paid ransoms for captives of terrorists and such payments have improved terrorist finances, supplies, status and operations, often prolonging the terror carried on by such groups. The US Government's policy is that it will not negotiate with terrorists.

From the US perspective, prisoners are primarily used for extracting information or providing leverage for financial or propaganda gain, which in turn can supply terrorists with the means to continue their fight. Looking more broadly throughout history and geography, we see POWs put to a range of uses. The millions of Soviet POWs captured during World War II were exploited by the Germans as an utterly expendable form of slave labour, and literally millions were worked to death or subject to casual execution. (The Soviets returned the bleak favour to some three million German POWs at the end of the war.) Prisoners have also been executed, sometimes *en masse*, as a kind of rite to prove the ideological 'purity' of the executioners. We have recently seen this most horribly demonstrated by fanatical Islamic groups in the Middle East and Central Asia, but the practice goes back to ancient times, particularly in the form of beheadings.

It would appear from this unnerving picture, and from the fact that many governments (like that of the US) 'will not negotiate with terrorists', that the POW is in a uniquely powerless situation. Yet while never downplaying the very real dangers, there are things a soldier can do to increase his chances of making it through, or at least prolonging his survival long enough for an escape or rescue attempt.

Surrender

Surrender to enemy troops is a precarious business, particularly if the troops have just been in combat. Keep your arms high and make sure that you are carrying no weapons of any description.

First Moments

The first moments of captivity are the most dangerous, as the captors will often be nervous with their new prisoner. Comply fully with any orders given, and don't make any sudden movements.

The First Moments

The first hours of being taken prisoner are the most dangerous of all for POWs. In the immediate aftermath of battle, trigger fingers are still itchy, hearts are still beating hard and the captors have no empathy with or understanding of their new charges. In fact, it might well be easier for them to kill any prisoners rather than go to the effort of protecting them and taking them back to a prisoner facility well behind the frontlines. Note that historically it is not just ideological fanatics who show reluctance to take prisoners on the battlefield. During World War II, the Surgeon General of the US First Army Group stated that 'American troops are not showing any great disposition to take prisoners unless the enemy come over in batches of 20 or more'. During the 1982 Falklands War, British soldiers were known to shoot down unarmed men at the immediate point the enemy surrendered, simply because it is hard to stop the process of killing once it is started.

Compliance

For the prisoner, compliance is key during the first few moments of capture. Bravado or defiance will likely bring you death or at least a beating or similar mistreatment. The latter may in turn leave you with permanent injuries that will prevent your future escape, so however much

you despise your captors, keep that attitude locked away inside your head. Be humble and calm, speaking in a low and unthreatening tone of voice and following any orders to the letter. Don't make any sudden movements, and don't make eye contact. Also, resist the temptation to beg or plead with your captors – this will likely attract more contempt than pity, and make them more not less willing to inflict harm on you.

An additional danger is the threat from local civilians, as they may well have suffered under the effects of your own side's artillery and air bombardments. Senator John McCain, as a young A-4 Skyhawk pilot flying combat missions over North Vietnam in 1967, experienced the full terror of being exposed to angry locals after he was shot down over Hanoi. Severely injured, he was pulled from a lake:

Some North Vietnamese swam out and pulled me to the side of the lake and immediately started stripping me, which is their standard procedure. Of course, this being in the centre of town, a huge crowd of people gathered, and they were all hollering and screaming and cursing and spitting and kicking at me.

When they had most of my clothes off, I felt a twinge in my right knee. I sat up and looked at it, and my right foot was resting next

69

Rough Treatment

In many conflicts, POWs have been paraded by their captors in front of crowds of hostile civilians. In these situations, keep your face down and shoulders hunched to protect you from blows to the head, and don't become separated from your captors – they are unlikely to want you to be killed, and are probably your best chance of protection.

Guard Dog Defence

If you are 'captured' by a guard dog, try to keep it at a distance with kicks. If it closes up to you and bites, it will probably go for your arm or leg, in which case try to strike it off with a blow to the head or eyes from a club.

to my left knee, just in a 90-degree position. I said, 'My God – my leg!' That seemed to enrage them – I don't know why. One of them slammed a rifle butt down on my shoulder, and smashed it pretty badly. Another stuck a bayonet in my foot. The mob was really getting up-tight.

There is obviously little that a person can do in such situations, apart from surrender to fate and rely on the questionable protection provided by the guards. They are likely to get in severe trouble if they allowed a potentially valuable prisoner to be murdered before reaching captivity.

Gathering information

During the first minutes and hours of captivity, you are not entirely helpless. Full knowledge of your situation and surroundings is critical, so without raising obvious suspicions, take in as much information as possible. Mentally ask questions such as:

- Who seems to be the leader of the group? The second-in-command?
- What is your location? Mentally take note of any prominent landmarks or street names around you – being able to identify this location might come in useful later on for a rescue or escape attempt.
- From the conversation amongst the captors, can you pick up any details about where you are being taken? Even if you don't speak the language, listen out for any familiar place names or regularly repeated words that sound significant.
- Do any of your captors appear to have physical or mental weaknesses, such as leg injuries or bullying by other members of the group, that you might be able to exploit later on? Conversely, these characteristics might also pose a danger to you, so they are useful to note.

In short, take in as much as you can before you are transported off to an unknown destination – you never know how the information will later be of use.

If you are held with a group of other prisoners, and have the chance to talk without being overheard, use this moment to share as much useful information as possible. (Be careful here – sometimes a canny enemy will implant a prisoner who is actually one of their own group, and who can listen in on what the prisoners have to say to one another.) A common interrogation and prisoner policy (unless extremely large numbers of prisoners are taken) involves separating all the prisoners from one another as soon as possible. This way the prisoners are unable to make

Tip: Dealing with your Captors

The US Department of Homeland Security offers this advice for handling your captors:

- Do not aggravate them.
- Do not get into political or ideological discussions.
- Comply with instructions, but always maintain your dignity. Obedience to orders or commands need not be swift, cheerful or overtly enthusiastic, but it should be sufficient to maintain a balanced relationship.
- Talk in a normal voice. Avoid whispering when talking to other hostages, or raising your voice when talking to a terrorist.
- Attempt to develop a positive relationship with them. Identify those captors with whom you can communicate and attempt to establish a relationship.
- Be proud of your heritage, government and military association, but use discretion.

common plans to resist or escape, and they are prevented from agreeing false stories that they can then present during interrogation. Therefore, use any opportunities while you are together to help each other, and provide some mutual support in what is a traumatic situation for everyone. If anyone appears to be panicking, speak to him quietly and reassuringly until he calms down. Any sort of loud or distressed behaviour can bring the guards' violence down on the whole group, so try to get everyone to a base level of calmness.

Government Prisoner

In this chapter, we will consider the two different scenarios potentially faced by a soldier, sailor, marine or airman taken prisoner. One is that he or she falls into the hands of a conventional government and military; the other is to be captured and held hostage by a terrorist or insurgent group.

POW camps

Looking at the conventional scenario first, the key difference between a regular army prison camp and a terrorist's cell is naturally one of scale. Conventional prison camps might hold literally thousands of men, of many different nationalities and units. Prison security will typically be tight (although not always, if the camp has been thrown

Assessing the Prison

On your arrival at a POW camp, evaluate every aspect of the security. Here we have a double fence arrangement, each fence surmounted by coiled razor wire and electrified cables. The ground between the fences is watched by troops on watchtowers, the sentries manning searchlights and machine guns. Floodlights cover the whole perimeter of the prison.

Deprivation

Keeping prisoners in total squalor is a method by which captors establish dominance over their prisoners. Keep an internal dignity in these circumstances, using a humorous and defiant inner voice to defy your captors.

up in a hurry), and will include features such as multiple perimeter walls; searchlights; watchtowers fitted with automatic weapons; large numbers of guards patrolling with dogs; and electronic escape alarm systems. As a prisoner in such a facility, you are unlikely to find yourself held in a cell on your own, unless you are confined to a isolation unit or have been deliberately separated from other prisoners on account of your special importance.

Large prison camps bring a certain degree of anonymity. (If you are an officer detained with fellow members of your unit, tell them to refrain from saluting you, as this will bring you to the attention of the guards.) Whether the anonymity of the camp brings benefits or problems depends very much on the institution and how it is run. In the most fair-minded camps, prisoners can be treated like sternly regarded guests.

Some German and Italian POWs held in Britain or the United States during World War II, for example, were given paid work on local farms and in factories and were even allowed out periodically to go to bars, restaurants, theatres and sports events. Many became close friends with local people, and even stayed in their forcibly adopted country after the war ended.

Yet equally, major prison camps can result in appalling brutality and neglect. Partly this can result from logistical reasons – large influxes of prisoners often overload both food supplies and administrative capabilities, fostering under-nourishment, starvation and overcrowding, and the concomitant disease that thrives in such situations. These conditions are exacerbated by racial or political enmities between guards and prisoners. Outright violence, torture and chronic mistreatment can become terribly commonplace. Examples of such treatment are legion throughout the twentieth century, and include recent examples of brutally run camps in the former Yugoslavia in the 1990s.

Relationships with the guards

Survival in these establishments undoubtedly requires a degree of luck, but there are more pro-active steps to give hope. First, maintain good relations with the guards, always being respectful but implicitly treating them as human beings (even if they don't deserve such treatment), and trying to identify common ground for understanding, such as concerns over family and money. Don't overstep the familiarity, but in time you might find a cordiality building up between you and a particular gaoler (as unpalatable as that might seem). This relationship could work to your advantage, especially if the guard displays a genuine humanity towards his charges.

Dealing with a Knife Threat

If attacked by another prisoner with a knife, try to grab the wrist of the knife hand in a strong double-handed grip and swing it across your body, throwing your opponent to the floor. Attack his eyes, throat or other vulnerable point to bring the attack to an end.

A remarkable example of a guard acting as carer comes from the Japanese prison camp system of World War II. John Baxter, a captured British soldier, endured an agonizing experience of forced labour in South-East Asia, working in mines and railways under tropical heat and the draining effect of diseases such as malaria and dysentery. Hundreds of men died, including from regular violent beatings and snap executions. Yet while the vast majority of guards were closed to mercy, Baxter found that there was one guard, Hyato Hirano, who retained his compassion.

While in front of his fellow guards he disdained the prisoners, delivering beatings of his own, but behind their backs he risked his own personal safety by providing food and water to the six prisoners over whom he had direct responsibility. He even smuggled in cakes that his wife had baked. Had Hirano's acts of kindness been discovered, he would have been executed. As it was, he helped Baxter and other individuals to survive the war.

Such cases of kindness can be a rarity in many POW camps – brutal cultures tend to drag everyone into

information. Basically, stay on your toes and try to obtain every advantage you can without breaking your loyalty to comrades and country. Furthermore, maintain your military bearing and dignity at all times – do not stoop to the low levels of many of those around you.

Surviving other inmates

It is worth acknowledging another potential danger in POW camps – other inmates. A large camp can hold prisoners from many different ethnic groups, with differing political ideas, behaviours and social backgrounds, not all displaying harmonious relations with one another. Furthermore, although the system of rank authority should technically be preserved in a POW camp, it is not uncommon for the formalities of military order to break down over time. Historian Dean B. Simmons conducted a lengthy study of the behaviour of German and Italian POWs held in Minnesota in 1944–45. The treatment of the inmates by the US soldiers was generally good, but within the German ranks there developed a division between veteran soldiers who had fought during the early years of the war, and more disillusioned latecomers. Such was the level of violence between these two groups, which included occasional murders, that the US authorities were forced to separate them into different camps.

them, either through complicity or weakness. In these situations, a prisoner has to seek out every advantage to avoid the worst attention. Try to get transferred to sections of the camp away from particularly aggressive guards. Demonstrating a skill of value to camp life, such as carpentry or metalworking, is another way to obtain minor favours and preferential treatment. Be careful, however, that such treatment doesn't come with lots of unacceptable strings attached to it, such as informing on fellow prisoners or giving away important

Safety certainly comes in numbers in these environments. Being part of a unified, coherent group makes you less of a target to more predatory members of the camp. Neither you as an individual nor the group as a whole should display any signs of weakness, which will simply open you up to exploitation. If physically attacked, you should reply in kind with all your strength; even if defeated, you will have proven yourself a 'hard target', and the aggressors will likely seek softer

Trade and Weapons

POW camps often have a lively trade in basic goods, particularly chocolate and cigarettes, and also anything that can relieve boredom, such as books. Playing a controlling part in such trade can help you surive the camp. Note also that the simplest of materials can often be turned into weapons with a bit of ingenuity, to provide you with some protection.

Goods for trade

targets in the future. Some prisoners will make all manner of improvised weapons to act as equalizers. These include knives made from pieces of sharpened plastic, sharpened toothbrushes and razor blades fitted to combs. As taught in police officer training, keep your eyes firmly glued on the hands of anybody you deem suspicious, and keep a safe distance from him at all times.

You should never encourage any antagonisms. There is enough danger from captivity alone without adding

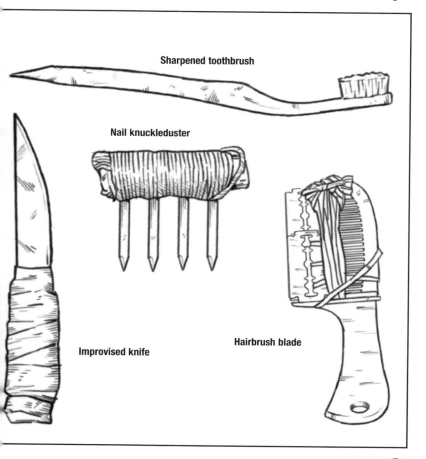

Sharpened toothbrush

Nail knuckleduster

Improvised knife

Hairbrush blade

Mental Interrogation

Interrogation is not always a brutal affair. Sometimes interrogators might use reason and argument to try to 'turn' a soldier to renounce his army's cause, often via distorted history lessons and biased social analysis.

internal threats, so attempt to build bridges between groups at every opportunity. Most camps develop some sort of internal 'economy', a trade in barter goods such as cigarettes, literature, food and soap. This trade in itself can produce tensions, particularly if it inspires thefts, but it can also give the prisoners a shared interest if run efficiently and fairly. Remember that you are all in the same boat, and by working together you can make it through the prison experience with greater morale and self-sufficiency.

Interrogation

Information is a prisoner's most vital asset to an enemy. Individually, a regular soldier might feel that he has little to offer in terms of high-value information. In reality, every scrap of data about the captors' enemies has some utility. A prisoner's casual comment about the types of food he ate back in his unit can, for example, give the interrogators insight into enemy logistics, or statements about leave rotas can indicate the manpower levels of a formation.

Rules when facing interrogation

In popular imagination, interrogation often involves a brightly lit room and heavy-handed efforts to beat information out of a resilient prisoner. This scenario indeed occurs, but intelligent captors have a far wider range of approaches available for

US Army Tip: Battle of Wills

Historically, the detainers have attempted to engage military captives in what may be called a 'battle of wits' about seemingly innocent and useless topics as well as provocative issues. To engage any detainer in such useless, if not dangerous, dialogue only enables a captor to spend more time with the detainee. The detainee should consider dealings with his or her captors as a 'battle of wills'; the will to restrict discussion to those items that relate to the detainee's treatment and return home against the detainer's will to discuss dangerous topics.

– CJCS, *Antiterrorism Personal Protection Guide: A Self-Help Guide to Terrorism* (2002)

extracting what they need to know. In 1944, the Royal Air Force produced a booklet for aircrews operating in the European Theatre of Operations (ETO), describing correct behaviour for a POW, should the airman be captured. The document advocates that an airman follow 'these simple rules when facing interrogation':

Telltale Signs of Lying

During interrogation, be aware of your body language at all times, in case it betrays that you are lying. Nervous rubbing of the face is often an indicator or a lie, and one that the interrogators will be trained to look for.

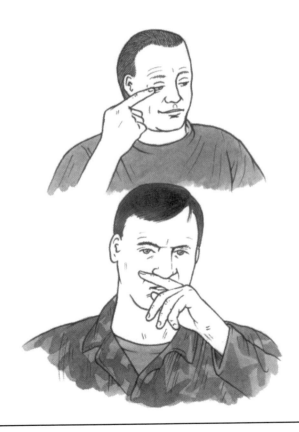

- *Stand correctly to attention;*
- *Give name, rank and number – and nothing else;*
- *Maintain a rigid silence thereafter, avoiding even the answers 'Yes' or 'No'. If pressed, he may reply 'I cannot answer that question';*
- *Avoid all attempts to bluff or tell lies;*
- *Preserve throughout the interrogation a disciplined and strictly formal attitude, addressing any officer senior to himself as 'Sir';*
- *Avoid all fraternization, and refuse all favours;*
- *Establish from the outset that he is a type from whom nothing can be learnt.*

Although dated, the essence of these rules still hold good today. In the Escape & Evasion & Tactical Questioning (TQ) training undertaken by the SAS, recruits are instructed to give only name, rank, serial number and date of birth, despite a range of physical and mental encouragements to disclose more.

The use of torture – as we shall see – can change the rules of the game, but the overall goal of providing nothing more than name, rank and number is a laudable one. It has, however, been expanded slightly in modern military guidance. The Department of Homeland Security manual quoted earlier states that 'In addition to asking for a US representative, detainees should provide name, rank, service number, date of birth and the innocent circumstances leading to their detention. Further discussions should be limited to and revolve around health and welfare matters, conditions of their fellow detainees and going home.'

These criteria are more broadly realistic than those given by the RAF. They implicitly recognize that modern POWs are unlikely to be captured in the huge numbers of World War II, and that each POW is likely to receive more personal attention from interrogators. They therefore give the POW leeway to talk more openly, but still cautiously, and thereby avoid a potentially dangerous crossed-arms confrontation with the interrogator.

Mixed approach

Note that good interrogators will not rely on a single technique exclusively, but will mix them up in the hope of catching the prisoner out with one particular approach. For example, during SAS interrogation training, the recruit will often experience hours of harsh treatment, ranging from standing immobile in stress positions to having female military personnel mock their physical attributes.

Once the ordeal is over, he might be thrown into the back of a waiting truck, where the driver engages him

Sensory Deprivation

Hostages are often placed in conditions of sensory deprivation, to disorient them and make them more dependent on their captors. This prisoner is kept hooded and with his hearing obscured by ear defenders.

in idle chatter. The driver is, needless to say, an interrogator himself, utilizing the prisoner's suddenly lowered defences to elicit a few scraps of information.

The essential point for any prisoner is to trust no-one outside his immediate circle of closest friends, and to be suspicious of anyone asking gently probing questions about his or her background or military service. Similarly, the prisoner should speak freely only in open locations away from the possibility of scanning microphones.

One way to test out the trustworthiness of a person or safety of a location is to give false information about some aspect of the prison, such as saying that you know where some alcohol is kept. If the information is acted upon by the prison guards – in our example, they might conduct a search of the location given – then you will know that what you said was betrayed.

Torture and Physical Coercion

Mark Baker's classic collection of Vietnam War memories, *Nam*, includes an anonymous account from a US airman who was captured by communist forces after his aircraft was shot down over a remote part of South Vietnam. Initially he was held by Viet Cong (VC) troops in native Montagnard villages, where he received no medical attention for his wounds, which included three broken vertebrae and severe burns. He was given little food and no warm clothing, and his weight dropped to around 41kg (90lb).

He was paraded in front of civilians and North Vietnamese Army (NVA) troops, in a crude display of belittlement, but it was only many months later that professional interrogators appeared. The opened their efforts by displaying their evident knowledge:

> They knew more about my area of operations than I did. They showed me that in an effort to make me break. They want things like photographs, tape recordings, broadcasts, signed statements, confessions that can be used for propaganda purposes ... They were good. They make our interrogators look sick. They were trained in psychology, steeped in Communist ideology and they spoke perfect English. They were three of them, two who did the actual interrogating and a political officer to keep those two straight.
> – Mark Baker, *Nam*, p.125

The interrogation sessions also included 're-education', essentially long-winded lessons about the history of Vietnam and the oppressions of foreign powers and capitalist ideology. The carrot of repatriation was constantly dangled

Royal Air Force Tip: Interrogators' Tricks

The RAF document does, however, go on to list the many tricks an interrogator can use to extract information, and this list is still absolutely relevant to interrogation scenarios today:

Fraternization
The commonest trick of all. Prisoners are well treated, entertained and given plenty to drink. An atmosphere of good fellowship is carefully built up and service matters are then casually discussed. A skilled interrogator will be present to guide the talk into the right channels.

Microphones
These are always extensively used, and are sensitive to the slightest whisper. Some will be so cunningly hidden that not even an expert can find them. Stool-pigeons, speaking perfect English and carefully briefed, will be introduced among prisoners. They will not be easy to recognize, and may even be the first to warn everyone of the need for caution when discussing Service matters.

Agents
The Enemy will have agents working among the nurses, doctors, attendants or guards who look after prisoners. These may either pretend to be sympathetic; or else pretend that they cannot understand English. Like the stool-pigeon, they will be good actors and very difficult to recognize.

Know-all approach
'We know everything already, so there is no point in your keeping silent.' It may be suggested that another prisoner has talked; or an

imposing-looking file may be produced which appears to give detailed information about R.A.F. units, aircraft, equipment and personnel, and may contain a number of photographs, newspaper cuttings and other such items.

Intimidation
A prisoner may be threatened, or attempts may be made to bully or browbeat him. A 'fake' shooting of other prisoners may be staged. Blackmail may be tried. Ill-treatment may occasionally be resorted to by the Enemy, even though the Geneva Convention forbids it. Attempts may be made to lower a prisoner's morale and to undermine his resolution by means of unsuitable diet: overheated cells; or solitary confinement.

Bribery
A prisoner may be offered preferential treatment, with special liberties and luxuries, if he will co-operate with his captors, either by talking himself or by persuading others to talk. A prisoner who collaborates with the Enemy in return for an easy life is a traitor.

Pressure Points

If you have to defend yourself against a serious attack, strike only at the vulnerable points of the human body, as illustrated here. Hitting large, solid muscle groups will have little effect.

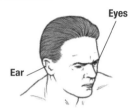

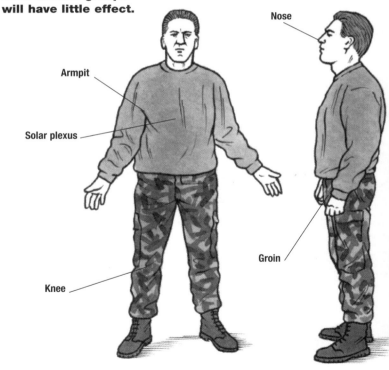

Eyes

Ear

Nose

Armpit

Solar plexus

Groin

Knee

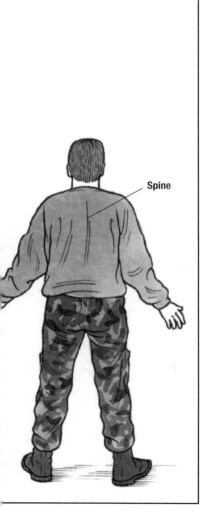

Spine

alongside the stick of threat, the interrogators stating that 'Once you understand the truth, we will release you to go home and tell the American people the truth of the situation.' The airman remained utterly unconvinced of the propaganda, but admitted that the promise of being sent home was a strong draw.

Torture

As often happens in the evolution of an interrogation, when mental strategies didn't work, torture was employed. (By this time the airman had been transferred to a prison in North Vietnam.) Infuriated by his continual defiance, the interrogators beat him severely and regularly, but had other, more medieval options. They would tie him up tightly with ropes in excruciating positions, and leave him there for hours. During one period he was forced into a cage that measured just 152 x 45cm (60 x 17in) and left inside for three months, simply for refusing to bow to the interrogators.

In the end, the airman was mentally and physically broken, and signed an anti-American propaganda statement. This act brought total self-loathing, but the person who can endure torture indefinitely is rarely, if ever, found. Former US presedential candidate John McCain also signed a similar statement after prolonged physical cruelty, afterwards observing that: 'I had learned what

Torture

Torture can take many forms, from verbal abuse (below), isolation (right) and prolonged exposure to extreme levels of noise (below right).

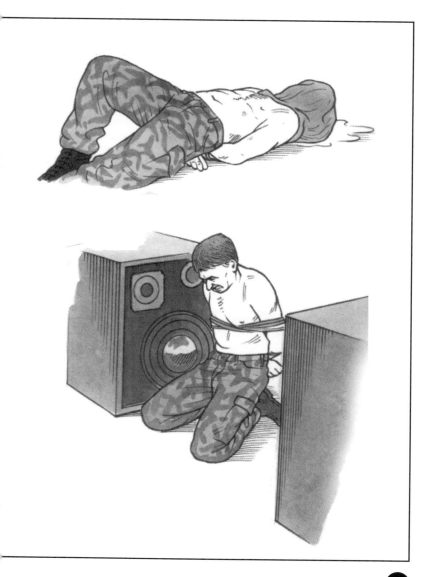

we all learned over there: Every man has his breaking point. I had reached mine.'

Remember that your own side will be equally aware of what information you possess, and what secrets you may be forced to give away, and so they can take measures to render your knowledge useless to the enemy. Indeed, some special forces soldiers, before embarking on missions, are given a list of genuine information they can tell the enemy if captured, but at a date that renders such information militarily useless. Platitudes and prescriptions about dealing with torture are, however, inappropriate to make by those who haven't experienced it.

Capture by Terrorists

In recent years, the world has been treated to a grim litany of hostage-taking stories emanating from the war zones of Iraq and Afghanistan. The tactics and outcomes of these incidents are not new to these conflicts, but they have raised awareness of the terrible dangers implicit in being taken hostage by an ideologically angry enemy.

As noted at the beginning of this chapter, terrorist groups have a range of uses for military hostages. They can be used as bargaining chips to obtain weapons or money, or the release of terrorist prisoners held elsewhere. They might be forced into making videotaped

declamations against their own country or military. Their lives might be threatened unless occupying forces leave.

A more appalling option is that the hostages are taken simply to be tortured and killed. On 20 June 2006, the beheaded bodies of two low-ranking US soldiers – Pfc. Kristian Menchaca, 23, and Pfc. Thomas L. Tucker, 25, of the 101st Airborne Division – were discovered after a three-day hunt by US forces. They had been captured by al-Qaeda terrorists following an attack on a vehicle checkpoint, before being tortured, executed and dumped. In customary fashion for al-Qaeda, much of the atrocity was videoed and released onto the internet.

Building a rapport

Such utter barbarity rightly appals us, and it would be glib to suggest that there is much a prisoner can do in such horrifying circumstances. If execution isn't the terrorists' primary or immediate goal, however, the prisoner should attempt to build a degree of human connection with his captors, in the hope of defusing some of the tension.

Creating a rapport with terrorists is not necessarily a pleasant process. Some empathetic techniques for getting to know your regular military captors have already been described above, and can be applied here, but attempting to associate with fanatical

Waterboarding

Although waterboarding has recently hit the headlines for its use in the so-called War on Terror, it is an ancient form of torture. It induces the sensation of drowning as the soaked cloth tightens over the victim's face.

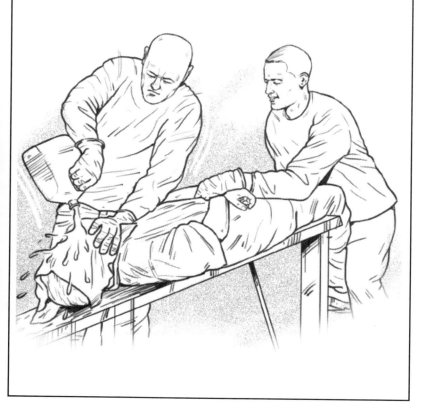

Human Trophy

Hostages have a value for their captors, either commercially or for propaganda. The most dangerous scenario for a prisoner is one in which the captors see him in ideological terms only, making him more liable to execution. A prisoner should therefore find every opportunity to increase the empathy between him and his captors.

terrorists is far more fraught with danger. Often they will see you as the living embodiment of an evil regime or heretical way of life. They may have lost relatives to the actions of your armed forces, or will have grown up in dehumanizing settings that have left them inured to violence. During the 1970s, when the world experienced an explosion of terrorism, many of the most radical terrorist groups emerged from the dire circumstances of the Palestinian refugee camps, in which an entire generation of children were born and brutalized.

The 'Building a Rapport' feature box below (see page 98) gives official advice from the Joint Chiefs of Staff for breaking down the barriers with hostage-takers. The point about 'Avoiding emotionally charged topics of religion, economics and politics' is particularly critical.

Terrorist members often have the deepest convictions about their faith and politics, and any arguing over these points will be a potential flashpoint. If you become the subject of a rant, or a terrorist attempts to draw you into such a conversation, be non-committal but listen attentively, to give the appearance of thinking carefully about what he or she has to say.

Be careful about making jokes because some points of humour, particularly in terms of sexual relations, do not travel well between different cultures.

'Stockholm Syndrome'

Do not take acts of friendliness too far. Becoming friends with your captor can cut both ways: it can be a source of protection but also a source of danger if for some reason you 'fall out' (arguments between former close friends are always the bitterest). In addition, FBI psychologists have acknowledged that about 27 per cent of people taken hostage (at least in civilian settings) show evidence of what is termed 'Stockholm Syndrome', where the hostages actually bond with the captors to an irrational extent. This syndrome is predictably the product of long-term incarceration, in which both captors

Tip: Building a Rapport

Hostages may discuss nonsubstantive topics to convey their human qualities and build rapport by:

- Introducing commonalties such as family, clothes, sports, hygiene, food, etc.
- Active listening. Allowing captors to discuss their cause or boast, but not to praise, pander, participate or debate with them.
- Addressing captors by name.
- Being careful about whining or begging, as it may increase abuse.
- Introducing benign topics at critical times (impasses, demands) to reduce tensions.
- Avoiding emotionally charged topics of religion, economics and politics.
- Avoiding being singled out by being argumentative or combative.
- Avoiding escalating tensions with language such as 'gun, kill, punish,' etc.

Antiterrorism Personal Protection Guide: A Self-Help Guide to Terrorism (US CJCS, 2002)

Boredom

Sheer, seemingly endless boredom is often one of the most difficult elements of captivity. It can develop into severe depression, which in turn often leads to inactivity and a surrender to fate.

Staying Fit

Staying physically fit is a great way of fighting off both depression and boredom, and also of giving the prisoner a greater sense of control over his own destiny. Exercise should not be excessive, however, particularly if the POW is suffering from poor health or inadequate nutrition.

and prisoners exist side by side in roughly the same conditions. The prisoner's perspective can be warped over time, and the absence of cruelty be interpreted as the presence of kindness. Remember that at some point your own forces might launch a violent rescue operation to free you. At that point, you cannot afford to have any divided loyalties.

Surviving Mentally

Before moving on to the issue of how to escape imprisonment, we need to address psychological strategies for coping with being a prisoner. Most accounts from ex-POWs emphasize the alternating fear, tension and mind-numbing boredom of captivity. Entire weeks, even months, of complete uneventfulness can be abruptly punctuated by sudden violence or mental tortures such as mock executions. Some coping mechanisms are needed if complete nervous breakdown is to be avoided.

At the start of a period in captivity, establish a clear sense of who you are and your importance in the world. Even though in prison, you still have a key place in the lives of your family and friends, and in the thoughts and efforts of your military unit. Return to this thought regularly to remind yourself that you are not, as prison life might lead you to

believe, a nameless, faceless unit in the system. Try to establish some sense of routine, however small and seemingly trivial it might be, because this will give you a degree of control over your environment, and make you feel less helpless. If you are imprisoned with others, make it a group responsibility to support one other at every stage.

Isolation

An especially cruel form of mental control involves putting a prisoner in prolonged periods of isolation. If the prisoner is held in a cell with no natural light, he will lose all sense of time, and the lack of human contact and anything to do can lead to psychotic levels of boredom.

The US airmen captured over Vietnam were often subjected to the most unbelievable periods of isolation. Of his five-and-a-half years in captivity, John McCain spent two of them in solitary confinement in a cell measuring 4.5 x 4.5m (15 x 15ft). He acknowledges that this isolation 'crushes your spirit and weakens your resistance more effectively than any other form of mistreatment'.

Similarly, the US airman quoted in Mark Baker's *Nam* stated that 'I didn't see or talk to another American for five years. That's one of the cruelest tortures.' In 1992, medical tests on 57 former POWs held in Yugoslavia during the war there revealed that many of them had brain abnormalities that were equal to the effects of traumatic head injury, but which had been inflicted purely through being kept in isolation.

Real time activities

Real-time mental projects are an important way of fighting off the sense of unreality that can come with isolation. Other mental regimes can involve revisiting happy memories in vivid detail; visualizing beautiful locations and going on 'holiday' there; writing a book in your head.

Whatever inventive technique works for you, go with it. Don't go so far into your mental creations that you then lose track of reality, however. Even after years in prison, you need to stay switched on to the opportunities for release, escape and rescue, as we will now explore.

Tip: Getting in Contact

If the layout of the prison allows, communication can sometimes be established with prisoners in other cells by tapping on walls and pipes. This dialogue might be frustratingly slow, but it can help to restore some sense of shared experience. Most important, however, is to replace what were physical routines with mental routines. An airman in Vietnam remembered that 'We all developed some sort of mental exercise':

I spent time designing my dream house that I would build someday. Then when I finally settled on the design, I decided to go ahead and build it. So I built it in real time in my head. I would spend a day with my eyes closed and in my mind I would be standing there supervising the bulldozers while they dug the foundations. If I figured it would take three days to get the foundation poured, I would spend three days actually working on the foundation in my mind. I built the whole house that way. It took about three months.
– Mark Baker, Nam, pp.125–26

Mental Life

In cases where a prisoner is isolated from others, he has to find interest within his own mind. Creating imaginary worlds, mentally writing books and solving logical or practical problems are all good coping strategies.

Escape from captivity should be the priority of any POW. Yet while Hollywood has given us many romanticized versions of escape adventures, the reality can be rather more discouraging. The fact remains that escape is extremely difficult, particularly once you are taken deep into an enemy prison camp system, or once held in a terrorist safe house. The captors will have committed time, money and intelligence to ensuring their prisoners stay locked inside, and they will constantly adapt and improve their security features and systems. Indeed, one point to bear in mind about escape is that each failed attempt generally results in tightened security, and reduced chances of future breakouts. This being said, history has provided plenty of examples of individuals who have defeated the cells, wire fences and watchtowers of seemingly impregnable institutions.

Early Escape

The first hours of captivity actually provide the best chances for escape. During the Korean War, some 670 US Army POWs made successful

....

A successful escape from captivity might involve precision skills such as lock-picking, or may demand simple violence to overcome guards or any others standing in the way of freedom.

3

Escape from a POW camp or terrorist holding cell can be a matter of either seizing a sudden opportunity, or of meticulous planning over a long period of time.

Escape from Captivity

Break for Freedom

If a soldier is captured on the battlefield, distraction can provide the best opportunity for escape. Here a prisoner makes a break for freedom while his captors are thoroughly absorbed in watching the effects of an air strike just metres from their position.

escapes from North Korean captivity, these comprising an impressive 10 per cent of the total US Army soldiers taken prisoner during the conflict. Yet all of these escapes were made from frontline aid stations or holding points shortly after the soldiers were captured; there were only 50 escape attempts from actual POW camps, none of which succeeded.

The US Marine Corp's manual *Individual's Guide for Understanding and Surviving Terrorism* iterates the advantages of early escape in the context of hostage taking:

> *Terrorists meticulously plan to capture hostages. Initiative, time, location, and circumstances of the capture usually favor the captors, not hostages. However, the best opportunity to escape is normally during the confusion of the takeover while you are still in a relatively public place. During this period the hostage-takers are focused on establishing control and may leave openings for escape.*

Although referring specifically to a terrorist action, this advice applies to all captivity situations. The first minutes of taking prisoners are often just as confusing for the captors as the captives, especially if the prisoners are taken unexpectedly during combat, rather than in a planned fashion. The sudden

Guard Attack

Using surprise and swift movements, it might be possible to disarm a guard by pulling his rifle barrel up or down (away from you) and wrenching it out of his hands (left and centre). Alternatively, attack a vital part of his body, such as the throat (right) with a spade or other tool, keeping the rifle barrel pushed to one side.

explosion of an air strike or artillery bombardment; the disruption caused by a vehicle hitting a mine; a firefight erupting – all these and similar incidents might momentarily cause your captors to refocus their attention elsewhere, and give you the opportunity to make an escape.

Try to do so only if you have a semi-clear plan of action in mind, meaning that you have somewhere to go and the real possibility of reaching friendly forces – don't just run away mindlessly. Also note that a disadvantage of immediate escape is that your captors will likely notice your absence within minutes, even seconds, of your escape attempt, unless the distraction stimulus is prolonged. (For example, if they find

themselves ambushed and in a fight for their survival.) Don't suddenly make a break for freedom because they are momentarily glancing away; you'll likely be shot before covering any distance.

Danger of violence

The USMC manual cautions about the dangers of this early capture

period, noting that 'Abductors are tense; adrenaline is flowing. Terrorists [and soldiers] themselves feel vulnerable until they are convinced they have established firm control over their hostages. Unintentional violence can be committed with the slightest provocation.' For this reason, early attempts to escape must have a very high possibility of

Opportunistic Escape

Here a prisoner makes an escape from the back of an enemy SUV while his captors are involved in a firefight. Attempt an opportunistic escape only if the captors are truly handling an extreme situation that demands all their attention and effort.

success, as failed attempts could result in automatic execution. This possibility becomes an almost certainty if you use violence against your captors to create an opening, although sometimes aggressive action might be warranted.

A violent escape attempt is a distinct possibility if the number of prisoners significantly outweighs the number of captors. Such a point was horribly proven in November 2001, at the Qala-i-Jangi fortress in northern Afghanistan. Several hundred Taliban prisoners were being held by Afghan Northern Alliance forces allied to General Abdul Rashid Dostum. Searches of the prisoners had been poorly conducted, and many of the anxious Taliban had concealed weapons about their person.

On Sunday 25 November, two CIA officers – Johnny Michael Spann and Dave Tyson – arrived to screen the captives for possible members of Osama bin Laden's al-Qaeda terrorist network. They did so in an open courtyard in front of a large group of prisoners, rather than processing them more manageably one by one, and their only protection came from a few Northern Alliance guards. During the interrogation, the prisoners suddenly rushed and overwhelmed Spann and the guards – Spann became the first American to die in combat in Afghanistan. The resulting general uprising at Qala-i-Jangi, in which the prisoners equipped

US Marine Corps Tip: Hostage Health

Typically, hostage-takers want to keep their hostages alive and well. Eat whatever food is available to maintain your strength. If you need medicine, ask for exactly what you need. If your abductors want you alive, they are not likely to take chances by providing you with the wrong medicine. A side effect of captivity for some hostages is weight loss. Although this may be considerable, it generally does not cause health problems. Hostages may also suffer gastrointestinal upset including nausea, vomiting, diarrhea, and/or constipation. Although these symptoms can be debilitating, they are usually not life-threatening.

– USMC, *Individual's Guide for Understanding and Surviving Terrorism* (2001)

Press-ups

Staying fit is an essential part of preparing for escape. The basic press-up is an ideal exercise for strengthening arm, upper body and core muscles, and can be performed in most confined spaces.

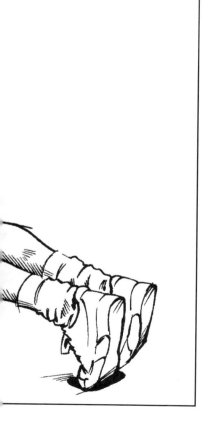

themselves with weapons from Dostum's own armoury, degenerated into a battle that ran until 1 December and killed some 300–400 Taliban and 73 Northern Alliance soldiers.

The grim case of the Qala-i-Jangi uprising shows how weak security arrangements can be exploited by prisoners to create an escape opportunity, although it also illustrates that the price of an uprising can be high for those who take it. (Spann himself managed to fight bravely with an AK-47 and pistol for a brief period of time, killing several Taliban before being overcome.)

For the vast majority of soldiers taken prisoner, early escape does not emerge as an option, and they are taken deeper into the enemy's prison system. For these individuals, escape requires far more than on-the-spot improvisation.

Ready for Escape

In the previous chapter, we explored some of the ways in which a soldier can survive captivity itself. Such measures of self-preservation are essential for any soldier intent on escape, for he will be able to do so only if he is fit and resilient. Breaking out from a cell or camp is just the beginning of the escape and evasion, and the attempt itself will be pointless if the soldier ends up collapsing, exhausted or ill, just a short distance from his prison. For this reason, a POW must integrate personal fitness into his escape plan. If you are held in a small cell for days on end, opportunities for physical improvement are naturally restricted. Yet even in these unpromising circumstances, a fitness regime is possible through the following compact exercises:

- Push-ups – improve strength of arms and upper body.
- Tricep dips – perform these using a bed or chair; improve strength of triceps and upper back.
- Squat thrusts – enhance cardio-vascular stamina and strengthen leg muscles.
- Lunges – improves power in the thighs.
- Crunches/sit-ups/leg raises – strengthens core stomach muscles.
- Running on the spot/star jumps – develops cardio-vascular endurance and greater stamina.

In addition to these, and similar, exercises, you can also use any available heavy objects – such as large books, rocks, bags filled with sand – to develop your own 'free-weights' routine.

Exercising during periods in the open yard are also invaluable, especially as they can take the form of morale-building team sports such as football/soccer or basketball (if the guards allow such luxuries). Not only do such sports have positive

Sit-ups and Crunches

Sit-ups and crunches are another compact exercise suited to keeping you fit for an escape attempt. By varying the angle at which you raise the upper body – such as with this oblique crunch – you can strengthen different parts of the abdominal muscles.

psychological effects, but they also provide you with an inconspicuous training regime. Excessive, solitary exercising might alert your guards to the fact that you are up to something, so try to keep your individual training programme private.

Do not overdo your exercise regime, however. If you are weak or ill, excessive training can exacerbate your condition. In such situations, you might be better conserving your energy until you actually need it, or postponing any escape attempt until you have recovered some vitality.

Planning

All escape planning begins with intense observation. This should begin from the very first moment a soldier is taken prisoner, and involves studying and memorizing every aspect of the environment and the prison system. Essentially the soldier is looking out for any weak links in security, plus any navigational information that might help him outside the wire. The covert reconnaissance must be an ongoing process, and should be part of a soldier's daily routine in the camp.

Information gathering

The types of information a soldier should attempt to glean includes the following:

- The exact configuration of outer security fences, including the locations of all gates and other entry points.
- The position of watchtowers and guard posts, and the field of view commanded by each.
- The times at which guards and sentries are rotated.
- The regular patterns described by searchlights, and the location of motion-activated lighting.
- Electronic security systems deployed around the camp, including closed-circuit televisions, thermal-imaging sensors, electric fences, motion detectors and alarm systems.
- The times at which routine events occur around the camp, such as meal times, the arrival of laundry, roll call, etc, and when the guards come on and off duty.
- The personal strengths and weaknesses of the guards, especially their intelligence and observational skills.
- The nature of the landscape around the prison, noting features such as approach roads, significant buildings, farmhouses and woodland. (This information is often gleaned on the journey to the prison, or on trips outside the camp when on work details.)
- The physical structure of all buildings, including windows, door locks, flooring, roofs, electric supply (note the locations of junction boxes), waste disposal facilities and water supply.

Distance and Area

With every metre distance you travel from the camp, the
area to be searched by the enemy grows exponentially.
A distance of 1km (0.6 miles) gives an area of 3km²
(1.6 square miles), but a distance of 2km (1.2 miles) gives
12.5km² (4.8 square miles).

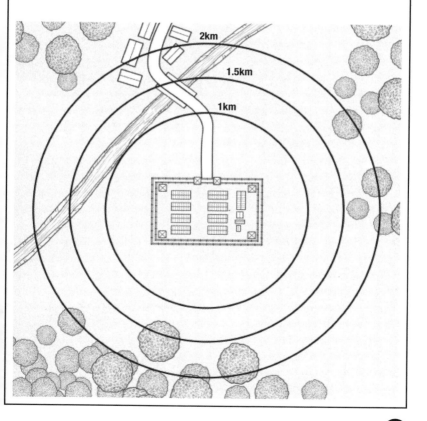

Security Challenges

This prison camp layout presents several challenges to anyone attempting to escape. The gap between the prison barracks and the outer wire is well covered by observation towers, and there is only one main gate into and out from the camp. The outer wire extends to a considerable height,

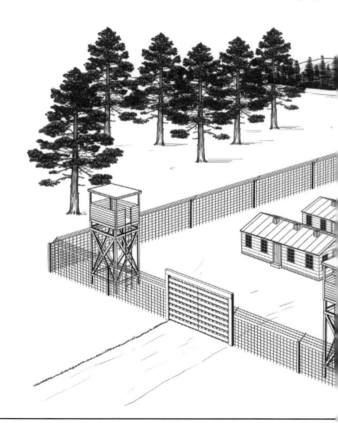

and has an overhanging configuration at the top. However, the barracks are closely packed enough for activity to go on between them unobserved from the towers, and if someone can get under the wire it is a short distance to visual cover in the nearby forest.

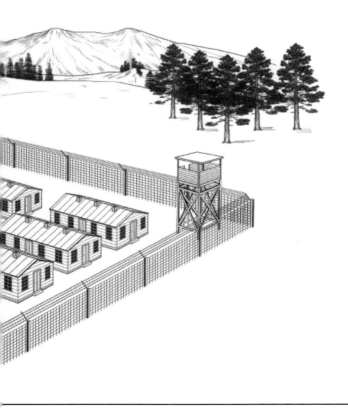

- The distances between all the key features in a camp – walk them out mentally.
- The locations of any places in the camp that could provide useful tools or equipment, such as an engineering workshop or arsenal.

In short, pay attention to everything about the physical and daily life of the prison where you are being held, looking for weak points in the defences and understanding exactly how the guards run the camp.

An excellent example of the observant POW comes from the testimony of two Slovak inmates –

Tip: Escaping Auschwitz

Alfred Wetzler explains the challenges of escape:

Escape through these two sentry belts is nearly impossible. To get through the inner belt during the night is out of the question, since the towers of the large belt are so close to one another (only 150 meters [137 yards], with each tower guarding a radius of 75 meters [69 yards]) that one cannot approach the belt without being observed. Anyone approaching is shot without warning. Relief of the guards in the big belt takes place at night only after the roster has been checked in the small belt zone, and it is ascertained that all prisoners are within that area. If, at the roll call, any prisoner is found missing, an alarm is given by sirens. When a prisoner is missing, the guards of the outer belt remain in their towers and the guards of the inner belt also take up their posts. Hundreds of SS men with bloodhounds search the area between the two guard belts. The sirens alert the whole region, so that even after miraculously breaking through the two guard belts the escaping prisoner faces the danger of falling into the hands of numerous German police and SS patrols. Escaping prisoners are greatly handicapped by their shaved heads and marked clothes (rags painted red). The population of the area is so intimidated that, at best, it is passive to escaping prisoners. Death is immediately meted out to all those giving any aid to an escaped prisoner, even to those who fail to report instantly the location of such a person.

Alfred Wetzler and Rudolf Vrba – who were held in the Auschwitz-Birkenau concentration camp during World War II.

The two men were some of the very few to escape from the horror of Auschwitz and make it into Allied hands, and their testimony was vital for putting together a picture of this grotesque institution. Wetzler provided the following account to Allied investigators:

The dwelling-area of the camp, that is, the actual concentration camp, covers an area approximately 500 by 500 meters [457 yards by 457 yards] in size. This zone is fenced off by two rows of concrete columns about 3 meters [9ft 10in] high. The columns are connected with each other by high-tension wires supported by insulators. Between these two fences, about 150 meters [137 yards] apart, there are watch towers about 5 meters [16ft] high, equipped with machine guns and searchlights. In front of the inner row of high-tension columns there is a barbed-wire fence. Touching this ordinary fence is answered by machine gun fire from the watch towers.

Within a radius of about 2000 meters [1829 yards] the whole camp is surrounded by watch towers at a distance of 150 meters [137 yards] from each other. In contrast to the guard installations called Kleine Postenkette, *which are described above, this system is called the* Grosse Postenkette. *The various factories and shops are located between these two guard belts. Watch towers of the small (inner) belt are manned only at night, at which time the double fence is also charged with electric current. Sentries of the small belt are relieved in the morning and the towers of the large belt are manned.*
– US National Archives and Records Administration

This description is a model of observational memory. It not only includes the key features of the camp security, including the locations of the fences, searchlights and watchtowers, but also the rotation patterns of the guards, the hours at which various outposts are manned and the precise distances between key features. The obstacles to escape are unnerving. The Nazi commanders and guards not only relied upon formidable physical structures to keep the inmates inside, they also had meticulous anti-escape procedures, such as the use of regular roll-calls and an effective system for mobilizing search parties.

Moreover, the last sentences of this quotation illustrate how fear itself – not only amongst the prisoners – can be a persuasive deterrent to escape.

Amidst the unbelievable brutality of Auschwitz, the Nazis naturally resorted to violent disincentives:

If a prisoner is not caught after three days, the guards of the outer belt leave their posts, since it is assumed that the prisoner was successful in breaking through both guard belts. If the escaped prisoner is caught alive, he is hanged in the presence of the entire camp. If he is found dead, his body is exposed at the gates of the camp. In its hands is placed a sign which reads: 'Hier bin ich.'

Later in this chapter, we will explore how Wetzler and Vrba made their escape from the Auschwitz camp. Suffice here to say that one of the key ingredients of their escape was their understanding of every detail of the camp, as displayed above. To consolidate their knowledge, they created a ground plan of the camp, which provided a conceptual guide by which they could plan their escape.

Indeed, as long as a map can be hidden successfully, it is a superb escape resource. Prisoners held for long periods of time find that their memories of the outside world in particular can degrade, so a map of the camp's location, created as soon as the prisoner arrives at the camp, can refresh those memories later on, when needed.

Useful equipment

While planning to escape, a POW needs to be receptive to opportunities to acquire or make useful pieces of equipment that might aid the breakout. The key point here is to disregard nothing, and think laterally. A small piece of stiff wire, for example, could be used as part of a lock-picking kit (or to jam a lock), or to bind up barbed-wire strands. Scraps of cloth could prove useful in creating an improvised disguise. A section of rubber car tyre might help you negotiate an electric fence. Thus, as far as is possible within the security regimes of the prison, you must try to become something of a magpie, collecting bits and pieces and storing them in a secure location (not necessarily in your cell or barrack, which are likely to be searched regularly). Tools such as saws or pliers are obviously more significant acquisitions, and tend to come from workshops. Great care is required here. Most prison guards will be all too aware of the value of tools to inmates, and so will keep careful inventories of what has gone in and out of the stores. Less care, however, is often taken over broken or worn-out tools, which might be reclaimed from refuse and restored to some manner of functionality. A short section of hacksaw blade, for example, could be tied to two wooden handles to create an improvised saw.

Improvised Grappling Hook

Escape equipment can be manufactured from the most basic of materials. Here an length of old nylon cord has been tied to a bent piece of iron to form a rudimentary grappling hook, suitable for escape over wire or for lowering yourself down from a window or rooftop.

The ingenuity that POWs display in creating escape equipment can reach impressive levels. In the United States during World War II, German POW 'escape committees' – special groups of people in charge of assisting escape attempts – managed to create all manner of official-looking paperwork using little more than carved potato stamps, pieces of cardboard, pots of India Ink and engraving plates made from pieces of linoleum. The documents produced included US social security cards, driving licences, military papers and other forms of ID, and

Lock-picking

Lock-picking needs practice and some basic tools to perform with confidence, but it is a skill with an obvious utility for escape purposes. To pick a 'Yale' type cylinder lock, you need two items: a slim, flat piece of steel to insert as a torsion wrench, and a hooked piece of strong wire to act as a lock pick. First, insert the torsion wrench into the base of the lock and apply pressure in the direction in which the lock unlocks. Now slide the pick in above the wrench. Yale locks work via a sequence of spring-loaded two-section pins that drop down into a cylinder. All of the upper-section pins need to be aligned above the cylinder for the lock to turn. Therefore, using the pick, feel for each pin in turn, and push each upwards until it 'sets' above the cylinder. For this to happen, you must keep up a constant pressure on the torsion wrench, which creates a slight misalignment between the cylinder and the upper pins and ensures that the pins don't simply drop down again as you move through the sequence. Once all the pins are set above the cylinder, the lock should turn and you can open the door.

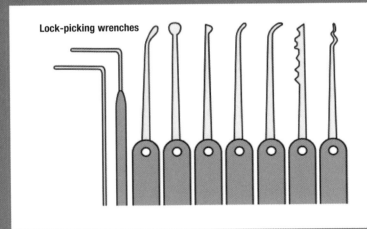

Lock-picking wrenches

Operating Yale-type locks

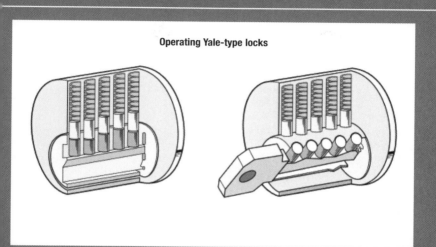

Lock-picking technique

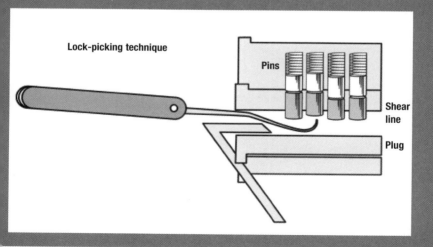

Pins

Shear line

Plug

these were used by many escapees to move across state or national borders (Mexico was a common destination for escapees), find employment or acquire money. (For more information, see www.U-boat.net.men/pow/escapes_us.htm)

A more spectacular creativity was displayed by six German POWs in a camp at Hearne, Texas. Under the vigilance of the US guards, they accomplished nothing less than building a sailing boat, forming a waterproof hull from stolen GI ponchos and using umbrellas for sails. This remarkable craft was used in an actual escape attempt; the six men were finally apprehended several miles down the Brazos River (they had been making for the Gulf of Mexico).

Such engineering flair is beyond many POWs, but escape is frequently a matter of thinking 'outside the box', and doing or making things inconceivable in the minds of the captors.

Many Minds

An important consideration for any escape attempt is how many people are involved. The equation can be complicated. The more people who know about the plan and are involved

Useful Tools

Tools such as pliers, hacksaw blades and files have an obvious utility for an escapee, although they will need to be hidden with absolute diligence in case of barracks inspections by the guards.

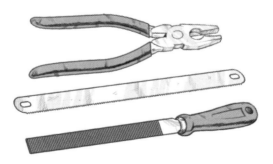

in its workings, the greater the chances that it could be revealed before being implemented. Yet complex escape plans – such as tunnelling operations – generally require multiple people to be viable at all, and the efficiency of the escape attempt can be improved by having many talented people working on it at the same time.

Often, the number of people involved naturally revolves around the members of a unit or squad. If working as part of an escape group, whether it is two or 200, ensure that each person has a clear role to perform, and also a coherent cover story if the attempt is exposed, a story that will prevent any investigation widening too far.

When putting together an escape group, you should also try to discover all relevant skills possessed by the group. In conflicts dominated by conscription or wartime voluntary enlistment, POW camps often held individuals who cumulatively had the full spectrum of vocational skills. A single barrack of British POWs in World War II, for example, might include former miners, carpenters, metal-workers, civil servants, administrators, scientists and (often usefully) former criminals. All such people have something to contribute to an escape attempt, from knowledge of how to dig a tunnel properly through to an understanding of how to 'age' documents with

natural materials. Linguistically talented individuals might also be able to deliver classes in the local language, improving the possibility of moving safely through towns and villages on the other side of the wire.

The Escape Attempt

Every escape attempt is unique, and attempting to lay down hard and fast rules to cover every eventuality is not possible. The nature of the escape depends upon the very experience of the camp. Camps with particularly brutal regimes often militate against carefully worked plans that take time to develop – the inmate spends most of his time and effort struggling to survive, and acts on basic plans that present themselves immediately. In camps where the prisoners are treated decently, the inmates might have the space to indulge more creative plans developed over weeks, months or even years.

Here we shall explore several different types of escape scenario through actual historical accounts, highlighting the pros and cons of each approach. We begin with probably the most advanced form of escape – tunnelling.

Digging to freedom

Tunnelling out of a prison camp has an obvious dramatic value, hence it has attracted considerable attention from the film industry. From a practical point of view, however,

Tip: Escape Networks

The value of having an escape support network is demonstrated by the following escape account, again from a German held in the United States in World War II. Tilman Kiwe, a major in the Afrika Korps, escaped on multiple occasions from US POW camps. Here he describes his third attempt:

It was not complicated to escape. The organization [escape committee] of the camp first obtained an American uniform for me that the guards must have traded for our military decorations or pretty wood sculptures. A tailor in the camp fashioned a very smart civilian raincoat. The problem was that it was grey-green, but we were not short of chemists in the camp. With boiled onions they obtained a marvellous shade of orange-yellow, and with tea they darkened it a bit to a perfect, inconspicuous color.

Before leaving this time I worked to perfect myself in English, especially in American slang. There was a prisoner in the camp who had spent 23 years in America; he was an interpreter and he took me well in hand. I could soon pass absolutely for an American ... Preparations were making progress. The organization had furnished me with the necessary money – about a hundred dollars ... The day was set for the escape ... I slid under a barrack. They were all on blocks; though there wasn't much room, I changed clothes, and stepped out in the uniform of an American Lieutenant. I waited until around 10:30 and went to the guard post. The sentinel must have thought I was taking a walk. I gave him a little sign with my hand, said 'Hello', threw him a vague salute, and hop! I was outside!

– Quoted in Arnold Krammer, Prisoners of War: A Reference Handbook (Westport, CT, Praeger, 2008)

Although captured two days later and returned to camp, Kiwe is to be admired for the sheer bravado of the escape attempt. Escape via disguise is an unpredictable business, and requires a huge amount of confidence and not a little good fortune to pull off convincingly. Kiwe's method of dressing as US military personnel was particularly high risk, as he could have been shot as a spy on recapture. Yet note how the various skill sets of the people around him contributed to his initially successful escape. Finding such broad talents is not always as easy in modern regular armies, in which many POWs will have few skills outside their military specialty, but enterprising individuals will typically find a way to achieve their goals.

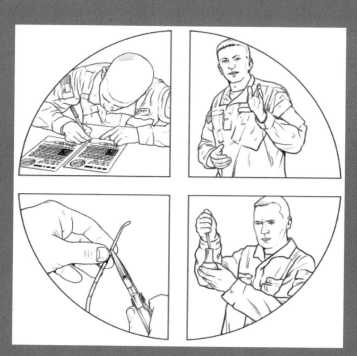

Tunnel to Freedom

This graphic representation of the tunnel dug out from Stalag Luft III shows how ambitious an escape attempt can become. The tunnel entrance is under the stove in the hut on the right, and it drops down to a workshop chamber below. Wooden carts were used to transport excavated soil back to the start of the tunnel.

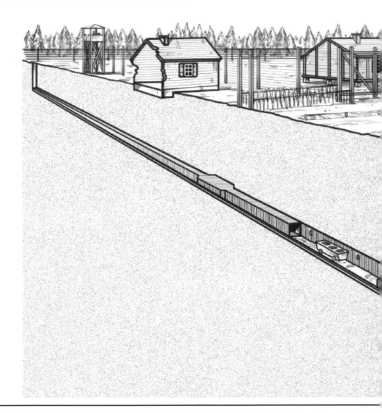

digging to freedom is one of the most difficult options. Yet as history has shown in some famous examples, it can be done.

One of the greatest of all the subterranean escape attempts was undoubtedly that conducted by Allied POWs held in the Stalag Luft III camp in Lower Silesia. The camp's security was formidably tight, and included seismographs implanted in the ground around the perimeter, to detect any signs of digging. Not dissuaded, the mainly British POWs formed an escape committee to look for ways to break out. Tunnelling was the chosen option.

The plan, devised in 1943, was for the prisoners to dig three tunnels out beyond the perimeter wire. Known as 'Tom', 'Dick' and 'Harry', these tunnels had to be deep enough to evade the German seismographic detectors, and long enough to go well beyond the perimeter wire into the surrounding tree line. Ultimately, only one of the tunnels – 'Harry' – was completed and used for its intended purpose, and it is worth a closer look to see how it was put together. ('Dick' was abandoned after its exit objective was covered by a camp extension, and 'Tom' was discovered by the German guards.)

'Harry' was 9m (30ft) deep and 102m (335ft) long by the time 76 men escaped through it as night fell on 24 March 1944. Its entrance was hidden beneath a heating stove

Tip: Tunnel Conditions

William Ash was one of 35 Allied POWs who escaped via a secret tunnel dug out from the Stalag XXI-B POW camp in Szubin, Poland, in 1943. Here he explains what the tunnelling experience was like:

We worked on in stifling darkness, trying not to think about the amount of unstable earth directly above our heads. It is hard to convey the sense of claustrophobia that comes from an hour of stabbing away at a wall of Polish mud so narrow that you can only get one arm forward to work on the face and which stretches back behind you so far that it takes half an hour to wriggle back to safety and sanity at the tunnel start. The experience assaults every sense. We felt the cold clay around us, pressing in on us and seeping into our bones until we almost became part of the tunnel. The loss of sight in the darkness when the lights went out was total. No glimmer of light had penetrated that wall of mud in a million years. Even when the margarine lamp flickered, it only served to emphasise the black.

– William Ash, *Under the Wire* (Bantam, 2005) p.213

(adapted to be movable) in one of the POW huts, and the initial shaft was dug down through solid brick and concrete. The frangible, sandy soil of the tunnel itself was shored up with bed boards and any scraps of wood that could be found. It was a narrow escape route, basically about 0.6m (2ft) square, but was worked to remarkable sophistication. POW engineers designed and built a bellow-like air pump that drove fresh air into the tunnel via ventilation ducts made from empty milk cans. Eventually the tunnels were fitted with electric lighting (replacing homemade mutton fat candles), running via stolen cable attached surreptitiously to the camp's electricity supply.

The tons of dug earth were transported along the tunnel in wheeled carts running along a wooden, rope-operated railway, and then disposed of furtively by hiding it in the legs of POWs' trousers – the prisoners would shake it out on the exercise ground, camp gardens, the camp theatre and any other suitable location. Two 'changeover stations' located along the tunnel – nicknamed 'Piccadilly' and 'Leicester Square' – allowed the tunnellers to switch from one cart to the next, and a workshop chamber was dug at the bottom of the entrance shaft, in which to perform essential engineering tasks.

'Harry' was an incredible achievement, more so when considering that the digging was performed by a mixture of stolen tools and other implements made from metal food cans and pieces of scrap. As is evident from the eventual inventory of items used by the tunnellers (see the box on page 134), the escape plan was a major logistical exercise, one that involved the cumulative cunning and

One-man Tunnel

This prisoner is escaping via a crude, unsupported tunnel dug out from his cell. Such tunnels require firm, clay-like soil to hold up without artificial supports, and shouldn't be dug too deep – the deeper you go, the greater the weight of soil pressing down on the tunnel roof.

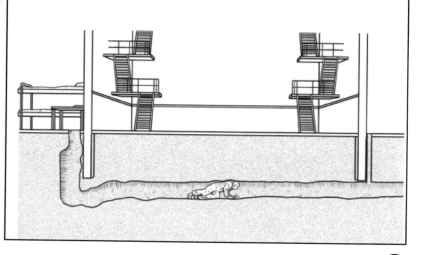

Inventory of Items Used in Digging the 'Great Escape' Tunnels

- 4000   bed boards
- 635   mattresses
- 192   bed covers
- 161   pillow cases
- 52   20-man tables
- 10   single tables
- 34   chairs
- 76   benches
- 1212   bed bolsters
- 1370   bedding battens
- 1219   knives
- 478   spoons
- 582   forks
- 69   lamps
- 246   water cans
- 30   shovels
- 328m   electric wire (1000ft)
- 180m   rope (590ft)
- 3424   towels
- 1700   blankets
- 1400   powdered milk cans

intelligence of dozens of men over a prolonged period. In addition, the escapees put together, stole or scrounged numerous other items that would help them on the outside – fake papers, currency, train timetables, civilian items of clothing – anything that would help them move through Nazi-occupied Europe.

The final escape of 76 men from Stalag Luft III was not, unfortunately, a story with many happy endings. Although a large number of men did make it beyond the wire, only three actually managed a 'home run'. The rest were captured and 50 of the daring escapees were executed, on Hitler's orders.

The price for what has become known as the 'Great Escape' had been very high indeed, but this action, and numerous other similar ventures, show its potential viability as an escape method. What follows are the key points to bear in mind when tunnelling:

- Distances from the start point to the exit point of the tunnel need to be accurately calculated, and the angle of the tunnel must be monitored at all times to ensure that the tunnel isn't wandering off course.
- The entrance to the tunnel needs to be somewhere accessible, particularly at night when much of the digging activity will take place, but there must also be a means of instantly and convincingly hiding it should guards conduct a search.
- Tunnels are prone to collapse, even in robust soils. Both walls and the roof have to be shored up and braced with materials strong enough to resist tons of pressure. If the tunnel construction takes place over a long period, these braces must be inspected regularly for damage from damp, cold or other phenomena.
- Earth disposal is a major factor. Remember that soils vary considerably in colour and consistency. Depositing sandy soil in a clay soil area, for example, could actually expose your digging activities, so choose your dumping location carefully. The issue of soil disposal is actually a reason why tunnelling escapes generally require large groups of people to perform, as the volume of waste produced is often too much to handle by a small group, unless a tunnel is particularly short. (The tunnel might not take you outside the wire, but just to another location within the prison from which it is easier to make the escape.)
- Tools are vital if you are to make significant progress with the digging. If you cannot acquire professional tools without raising alarm or suspicion, there is

Tip: Areas of Weakness in POW Camp Security

- Poorly maintained perimeter fences, including holes and rust-weakened sections.
- Low morale amongst the guards, resulting in a lack of vigilance during certain hours.
- Guards who are susceptible to bribes.
- External civilian workers (especially groups whose composition changes frequently) making regular visits to the camp.
- Lack of rigorous roll-call procedures.
- Poor-quality lighting at night, or blackout because of enemy aerial activity.
- Exposed electrical junction boxes, raising the potential for cutting power at opportune moments.
- Poorly guarded store areas containing potentially useful tools.
- Slipping out of the camp in trash trucks or other vehicles.

always the possibility of making them. Plaited strips of fabric can become ropes. Flattened metal cans attached to sticks can be spades. Fruit crates can be soil containers. Use your imagination, but make sure that any tool made is fit for purpose, otherwise you run the risk of injuring yourself.

- Ventilation is important in lengthy tunnels. Natural gases such as methane (produced by the decomposition of organic materials), carbon monoxide and carbon dioxide can build up in tunnels, and pose a threat to health. Some system is required to pump fresh air down into the tunnel. Watch out for symptoms of gas exposure, such as unusual drowsiness. If gas is suspected, limit the amount of time spent in the tunnel, or avoid it altogether.

Tunnelling is an ambitious enterprise, and its viability depends on many logistical and practical conditions. Yet for most escapees, more opportunistic above-ground methods of escape are required.

Above-ground escape
'Above-ground escape' essentially refers to any method of defeating a

camp's security system without digging beneath it. The list of methods here are potentially limited only by the imagination, so an exhaustive description of all possibilities is impossible. Nevertheless, we can detect common patterns of escape method within the history of POWs.

The case of Tilman Kiwe outlined above (pages 128–129) shows how a disguise and huge confidence can be one route out, albeit a dangerous one. Dressing up as either a foreign civilian or enemy soldier requires, first of all, that you acquire the necessary clothing. Authentic enemy uniforms are likely only obtainable from camp stores or secret suppliers (such as bribed guards), but sometimes your own uniform, stripped of rank insignia, straps, etc, can be given a

civilian appearance. Try to acquire any useful items of clothing as you spot them, such as hats, spectacles and scarves – these can be used to alter or hide your actual appearance should you make it outside the camp.

For another escape attempt, Kiwe explained that 'For three months I let my beard grow, and I completely transformed my appearance; I now had lacquered hair, parted in the middle, and glasses. And a real civilian suit this time. And, in order not to make the same mistake twice, I obtained a real American suitcase, so I would look less like a foreigner …'

The change in hairstyle is an easy way to distort your appearance, and growing it longer than usual can give you options for a variety of styles on a day-by-day basis.

Improvised Rope

Multiple strands of fabric twisted and knotted together can form a basic improvised rope for an escape attempt. Make sure that you test such a rope for breaking strength before using it in earnest.

Tackling a Guard

Here the escaping POW creeps up behind a guard, staying low (A). At the right moment, he leaps forward onto the guard's back, using momentum to knock the guard to the floor (B). As the guard falls forward, he will usually release his grip on his weapon to stop himself slamming into the ground (C). Once he is on the floor, the POW can render him unconscious with a stranglehold (D).

A

B

C

D

Of course, attempting to bluff your way out of the front gate requires nerves of steel, some capacity for acting, plus a high degree of knowledge. You will need at least a conversational grasp of your captors' language, including military terms, and of the local civilian language (if different). You should know the enemy's rank insignia system, to be able to salute when appropriate (if you are pretending to be an enemy soldier), and try to memorize any formalities or processes adopted at checkpoints. Avoid eye contact, however, and give an appearance of busy authority, which will reduce the risk of challenge.

Another identity you could adopt is that of an external contractor working within the camp, but you will need to acquire the necessary tools to give your lie some visual conviction.

Scissor Strangle

The scissor strangle is a chokehold that can be used to render someone unconscious quickly. Cross your wrists, grap opposite lapels, then pull your hands towards each other, pressing the wrists against the throat.

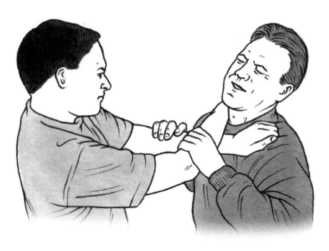

Any escape, as noted at the beginning of this chapter, begins with observation and the detection of a weak point in the camp defences. Alfred Wetzler and Rudolf Vrba – the Slovak inmates of Auschwitz-Birkenau mentioned earlier (pages 120–122) – managed to achieve exactly this in April 1944, when both escaped. They had spotted a large pile of timber lying just inside the camp perimeter, to be used in the construction of a new part of the camp. Slipping away one night, they hid beneath the logpile and stayed there for three days and nights while the German hunt for them played itself out. Once the initial surge of activity had died down, they emerged from the logpile at night, slithered through a hole in the fence and began a highly dangerous 128km (80-mile) journey through occupied Poland. Living rough, and sometimes

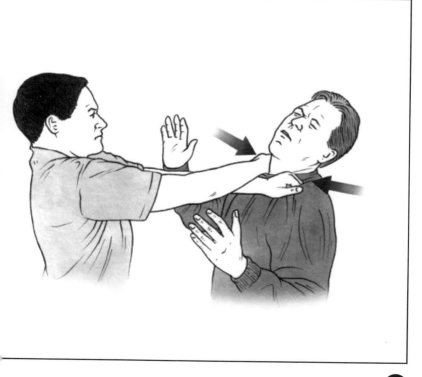

Team Work

Although an individual escape is least conspicuous, an escape team is useful when it comes to handling obstacles, such as this high wall here.

Operation Olympia

On 30 August 1942, 30 British and Allied troops made an audacious escape from the Oflag VI-B POW camp in the town of Dössel in north-west Germany. Using bed slats, they constructed four 3.6m (12ft) ladders in advance of the break-out attempt, ladders that featured extensions to enable the climbers to cross the perimeter wire and drop down safely on the other side. (The ladders could be disassembled to form bookshelves in their camp barracks, to avoid suspicion.) On the night of the escape, the escapees fused the camp lights and then rushed out to place the ladders against the wire, ten men to each ladder. One of the ladders collapsed, but 30 men made it to the outside world, although only three managed to evade later capture.

relying on the kindness of strangers, they eventually made it to safety, and brought with them evidence of the monstrous crimes being committed against the Jews.

Looking again at the figures for German POWs in the United States, post-war research showed:

Sixty-five percent occurred by getting through, under, or over the stockade fence. This included tunnelling, slipping through the gates in trash containers, hanging beneath trucks and jeeps, and every imaginable scheme in between. The second category, comprising 30 percent of the escapes, occurred by leaving work sites, by diverting the guard's attention, hiding among the

agricultural produce, or simply walking away. The remaining 5 percent were listed by the War Department as 'Miscellaneous', and generally comprised those escapes which occurred without the knowledge of the camp commander and came to light only on the capture of the escaped prisoner. –www.uboat.net./men/pow/ escapes_us_2.htm

These figures illustrate how simply grabbing an opportunity is often the most practical form of escape plan. For this reason, from the outset of your imprisonment you should have a clear idea of how to develop your escape once beyond the perimeter wire, in case you find yourself there at very short notice.

Uprising

Another, very different, method of escape is the uprising. In reality, a mass uprising and breakout at a camp is a last resort, bred by desperate circumstances. Threatened by violence and a mob, guards will typically open fire with all the weaponry at their disposal, leading to mass casualties. The breakout plan accepts this outcome, but works on the basis that a significant portion of those involved in the uprising will still manage to make their way to freedom. The balance can be tipped slightly in the escapees' favour if they manage to get hold of small arms themselves.

The case of Qala-i-Jangi, discussed earlier in this chapter (see pages 111–113), is one example of such an uprising. Another famous incident occurred at the Cowra POW camp in Australia during World War II — and illustrates the dangers. The camp held a mix of Italian, Japanese and Korean prisoners, and on 4 August 1944 up to 1000 Japanese troops rose up against their captors. They were armed with improvised knives, baseball bats, nail-studded clubs and other weapons, and surged against

Assault Deployment

These special forces soldiers use a fast-rope technique to deploy by helicopter during a POW rescue mission. Prisoners should prepare themselves for possible rescue as soon as they hear helicopters move in close.

and over the perimeter fence.
Although dozens were cut down by
machine-gun fire from Australian
guards, some 359 POWs managed
to escape. Within 10 days, however,
all had been recaptured. In total,
339 Japanese soldiers were killed or
wounded during the whole episode;
four Australians also died.

Uprisings tend to produce poor
rates of success for those involved.
This means that they should be
attempted only if the consequences
of not making the attempt are far
worse, or if the security of the camp
has been fatally comprised to the

extent that the POWs will easily gain
the upper hand.

Rescue

One other option for escape from a
POW or hostage situation does not
involve any effort on the part of the
prisoner at all – the rescue mission.
Rescue missions have varied
considerably in size. Examples of
large-scale actions include the
successful US mission to free 552
Allied POWs from the Japanese camp
at Cabanatuan City, Philippines, on
30 January 1945, and the airborne US
special forces raid against the Son

Rescue Bid: Clearing a Building

During a hostage-rescue action, a special forces team will work through each room methodically, often using stun grenades to soften up any opposition before entry. As they approach your room, announce your presence verbally, but stay in one place and allow them to come to you, unless doing so increases your danger.

Tay prison camp in North Vietnam on 21 December 1970. (The latter was a tactical success, with dozens of North Vietnamese guards killed, but all the US prisoners had been moved prior to the raid going in.)

Such bold rescue operations are quite rare because they have highly unpredictable outcomes. The hostage-rescue mission, by contrast, is more commonly attempted, as it involves more practical numbers of people to be rescued.

For those POWs or hostages who find themselves the subject of a rescue mission, the first moments actually represent a period of increased danger. Suddenly finding themselves under attack, terrorists or guards might attempt to kill their prisoners in an act of vengeance. Furthermore, there is a danger from the rescuers themselves, who are often fighting for their own lives and having to make split-second shoot/don't shoot decisions. On 8 October 2010, for example, British aid worker Linda Norgrove was killed by a grenade thrown by a member of the US SEAL team that was attempting to free her from a Taliban hideout in mountainous Afghanistan.

The first sign of a hostage-rescue action is often dramatic because the special forces will maximize shock value to overwhelm the captors. Stun grenades detonating, heavy small-arms fire, even air strikes – all can signal the beginning of the rescue attempt. If you as a prisoner become aware of a rescue mission unfolding, take the following actions:

- Get down and find a place of cover – there may be a lot of shooting around you in the next few minutes.
- Don't move about unnecessarily – ideally let the rescue forces find you, unless you are in a very isolated location.
- Don't pick up a weapon and attempt to join in – there is the likelihood that the rescuers could see you as a hostile.
- When the rescue troops find you, identify yourself quickly and simply, such as stating 'US citizen'. Don't be surprised, however, if you are roughly handled – the rescuers will treat you as a potential threat until you are clearly identified.
- Follow the rescue team's instructions to the letter.

Escaping from a prison camp or hostage situation is a perilous business. And if you do make it across the wire, you will then have to survive in hostile territory, which is the subject of our next chapter.

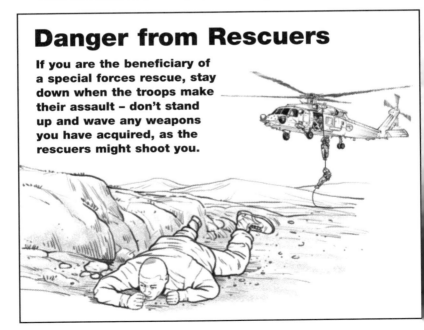

Danger from Rescuers

If you are the beneficiary of a special forces rescue, stay down when the troops make their assault – don't stand up and wave any weapons you have acquired, as the rescuers might shoot you.

Special Forces Rescue Team

A special forces hostage-rescue team will move at speed through a building, having to make snap shoot/don't shoot decisions. If the team is there to rescue you, be prepared for the detonation of stun and smoke grenades and for the use of heavy automatic firepower.

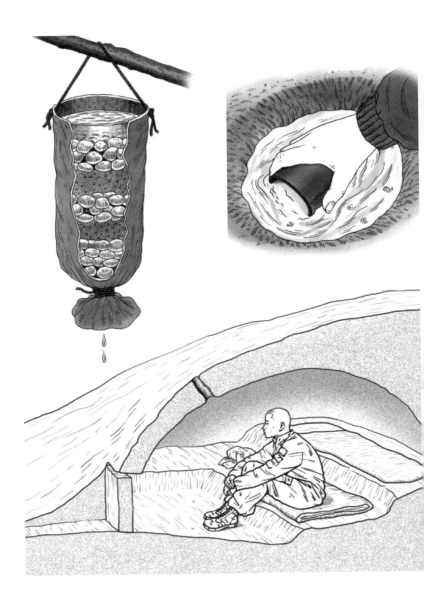

It is ironic that the greatest threat to any individual attempting escape and evasion might come from the environment, not from the enemy. In fact, the dangers presented by climate and terrain are considerably magnified when someone is on the run. For a civilian undergoing a survival challenge in a peacetime setting, the overwhelming objective is to increase his visibility to aid detection, and to make human contact as quickly as possible. Once he makes that contact, he can then surrender much of his responsibility for his own safety. The evader, by contrast, must largely avoid human contact – at least until he or she reaches friendly lines – and so must cope with every survival threat entirely on his own.

This chapter focuses on the core principles of staying alive in the wilderness, while at the same time staying hidden from an observant enemy. The last point is critical, and changes the survival game entirely. In a peacetime survival emergency, for example, it might be entirely appropriate to build a roaring campfire for warmth and cooking.

• •

Wilderness survival is usually taught as part of the basic training of most soldiers. The techniques acquired also have to be backed by improvisation and an unquenchable desire to live.

4

The most cunning and well-planned escape attempt can end in disaster if you aren't able to survive in the wilderness outside the POW camp.

Survival on the Run

Tip: Survival Kit

The actual contents of the survival pack can vary subtly according to the theatre of deployment, but the following list from an official US manual provides a good general outline:

In your survival kit, you should have:

- First aid items.
- Water purification tablets or drops.
- Fire-starting equipment.

- Signaling items.
- Food procurement items.
- Shelter items.

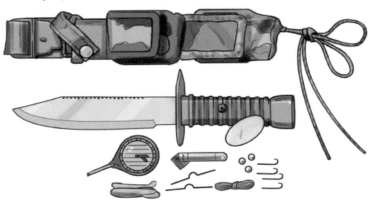

Special forces' multipurpose knife, which includes (inside the handle): a compass, fish hooks, flint/striker, fishing weights and line.

Some examples of these items are –

- Lighter, metal match, waterproof matches.
- Snare wire.
- Signaling mirror.
- Wrist compass.
- Fish and snare line.
- Fishhooks.
- Candle.
- Small hand lens.
- Oxytetracycline tablets (diarrhea or infection).
- Water purification tablets.
- Solar blanket.
- Surgical blades.
- Butterfly sutures.
- Condoms for water storage.
- Chapstick.
- Needle and thread.
- Knife.

Medical kit

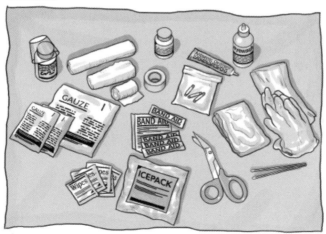

Do the same behind enemy lines, and the fire could act as a glaring locator beacon for an enemy search party, or could bring down artillery or mortar fire. The needs of survival must always be balanced against the needs of escape. Note, however, that it is pointless to stay on the run if it simply results in your death from starvation or hypothermia. *In extremis*, you may have to surrender.

Taking Stock

Most military personnel are the beneficiaries of some degree of survival training. This training, plus your natural intelligence and the will to survive, are the key factors in staying alive. Hopefully you will also have a survival pack – either official issue or one put together by yourself. Permanently carrying around such a pack might be one of the best investments you make.

The contents of the pack should be composed with clear survival objectives in mind: obtaining drinkable water; gathering food; starting a fire; signalling for rescue; making a shelter; and treating yourself if injured. If you have no such kit with you, life in the wilderness is going to present a considerable challenge, but with knowledge and willpower you can still adapt and survive.

Before making any decisions in the wild, it is important to think intelligently about all your actions

Water Sources

In an arid landscape, underground water is often often found under the soil on the outside bends of dried-up rivers, particularly if those bends spend much of the day in the shade. Water might also be found under rocks, such as those at the bottom of run-off channels in cliffs.

and their potential consequences. Carry out an immediate risk assessment, and identify what are the greatest threats to your well-being. For a pure survival point of view, you have a short list of priorities. Simplified to their extreme,

Locations that may contain water

these consist of the following: 1) Find water; 2) Find food; 3) Make shelter. The order of these priorities will vary according to your personal circumstances, but no element can be neglected without good reason. Here we will look at each in turn.

Water

Obtaining clean drinking water is paramount in any survival situation. If you have just escaped from a POW camp, chances are that you won't be carrying bulky water supplies, and therefore you have a

Tip: Water Containers

If you manage to obtain containers in which to carry your water supplies, note the following official US Army advice about storing water in hot climates:

Maintaining safe, clean water supplies is critical. The best containers for small quantities of water (5 gallons [22.7 litres]) are plastic water cans or coolers. Water in plastic cans will be good for up to 72 hours; storage in metal containers is safe only for 24 hours … If the air temperature exceeds 100 degrees Fahrenheit [37°C], the water temperature must be monitored. When the temperature exceeds 92 degrees Fahrenheit [33°C], the water should be changed, as bacteria will multiply. If the water is not changed the water can become a source of sickness, such as diarrhea.

– Field Manual 90-3, Desert Operations; US Army Survival Manual

problem. On standard operations, a soldier's water consumption needs vary from about 2 litres (4 pints) per day in cold climates through to 12 litres (25 pints) in extreme desert environments. If the fluid intake dips below the levels required to replace natural fluid loss (via sweating, urination, defecation, breathing, etc), then dehydration sets in. The consequences of dehydration range from mild mood changes through to death – without any water whatsoever, a person will be lucky to survive 3–7 days. One general important point to note is that you shouldn't eat if you don't have anything to drink, as the processes of digestion consume much of your body's water, particularly when assimilating fatty foods.

Geography and climate will generally dictate the availability of water. If you find yourself in a cold or temperate wilderness, there is likely to be plenty of accessible water in streams, rivers, puddles, snow (which should be melted before consumption), ponds, irrigation trenches and so on, although the open access to water doesn't avoid the need to purify it before drinking. When it rains, collect as much fresh water as you can in whatever containers are available – you can create 'gutters' into the containers by using thick leaves or pieces of waterproof fabric.

Yet during the summer months, or in arid areas, many natural water

Water from the Ground

When digging for undergound water, keep digging down until the soil turns damp and water starts to seep into bottom of the hole. You can scoop out any water collected, but make sure that you filter and purify it before drinking.

Dew Collection

A quick way of collecting dew from grass is to tie pieces of fabric around your ankles and then walk through the grass until the fabric is soaked. At this point remove the fabric, wring the water out into a container, then tie the fabric back around the ankles and repeat the process.

SURVIVAL ON THE RUN

sources can dry up, meaning you have to use more innovative ways of finding water. The following are some useful methods:

Dew collection

In the hours around dawn, when grass is wet from dew, rub a piece of absorbent fabric through the grass. The fabric will then become soaked in the dew, and you can wring the drinkable water straight into your mouth or into a container. Wrapping the cloth around your ankles and walking through the grass enables you to keep on the move at the same time as collecting water.

Hidden water

An arid wilderness might look barren, but water evaporates at different rates from different locations, according to its exposure to direct sunlight. There are many places in which water can collect and remain, particularly:

- Rock crevices, especially those with vegetation growing around them, or with spatterings of bird dung (indicating that birds have likely been there to drink).
- Plants with cup- or bowl-like structures, although you should never drink such water from poisonous plants, or if the fluid inside has a milky or otherwise discoloured hue.
- The crotches of trees, or holes in a tree-trunk – insects are often

seen moving in and out of these locations if they contain water.
- Dried river beds or waterholes – dig down into the angle of the most shaded bend (the last place from which surface water will have evaporated). If you find the soil becoming significantly damp, dig down further and let water seep into the hole for collection.

Solar still/transpiration bag

Making a solar still is a more complex method of acquiring water, and is possible only if you have or can acquire a quite large sheet of plastic. First find a sunny location and dig a hole 90cm (3ft) across and 60cm (2ft) deep, with sides slanting down to a sump in the centre of the hole. Into the sump place a water-collecting container, then lay the plastic sheet over the top of the hole, securing it around the edge with sand, dirt or rocks. Most importantly, make sure that you leave no gaps around the edge of the sheet, otherwise any water collected inside the still could simply evaporate through the gap and into the air. Also place a stone in the centre of the sheet, making the sheet dip down about 40cm (16in) below the ground level, over the collection container at the bottom.

The solar still is now ready to work. Leave it about 24 hours. As the sun raises the overall temperature within the hole, water vapour is released from the soil and condenses on the underside of the plastic sheet. This water then runs down the sheet to the lowest point and drips off into the container. If you have access to seawater, you can pour some of the fluid into the soil to increase the production of water vapour (the process of evaporation leaves behind the water's salt content).

A variation on the solar still is the transpiration bag, which works by extracting the water vapour contained in plants. Cut a large portion of green, living foliage from a tree or herbaceous plant and then seal it inside a plastic bag. There should be enough vegetation inside to fill three-quarters of the bag's volume. Tie the neck of the bag tightly, and make sure that the bag doesn't have any moulding holes in its base, which will let water escape into the atmosphere. Also place a small non-absorbent stone inside – lay the bag on a sunny slope, and work the rock down to the lowermost corner. As the sun warms up the bag, the vegetation releases its moisture, which again condenses on the plastic and collects at the bottom corner, where the rock is positioned.

The above methods of extracting water from the air or from plants are not always effective, and can have unpredictable results. Yet if properly executed, and in ideal conditions, they can produce in the region of 0.5–1 litre (1–2 pints) of ready-to-drink fluid every day.

Filtering and purifying water

Apart from the exceptions noted, and fresh rainwater, most water that you collect will need to be filtered and purified. This applies particularly to water collected from rivers and streams, which might look clear but which will often contain bacteria, parasites and organic materials invisible to the naked eye. These elements, if ingested, can cause diarrhoea, sickness and other diseases that actually accelerate body fluid loss. If you have no choice but to drink straight from a stream or river, the best types are those running over a bed of small stones, which serve to catch many of the impurities. Another less risky water source is underground water that bubbles to the surface through rocky ground; again, if the water looks clear, you can drink it in an emergency, but the better option if possible is always to filter and purify it.

To filter water, you can simply pour it through a piece of tight-woven material, such as a cotton T-shirt. A more sophisticated approach is to construct a filtration machine. This device basically consists of a funnel of material, tied at one end and filled with *contrasting* layers of natural filtration materials, such as sand and stones of varying sizes. Pour in water at the top, and the water that emerges from the bottom will be well-filtered during its passage through the layers. To purify the water, the simplest way

Solar Still

The secret to making an effective solar still is to make a watertight seal between the outer edge of the plastic sheet and the rim of the hole. To make drinking the collected water an easier process, you could also fit a drinking tube running down into the water container.

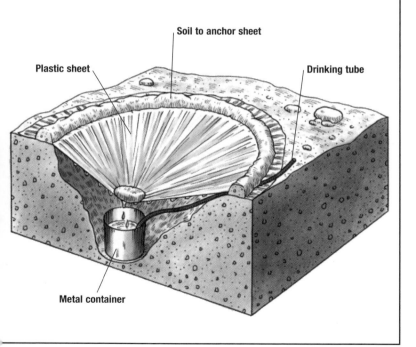

Soil to anchor sheet

Plastic sheet

Drinking tube

Metal container

s to add the water filtration chemicals n your survival pack, according to heir instructions. If you don't have these, make a fire and put the water through a rolling boil for about five minutes.

Tip: Jungle Water Sources

Jungle vines contain water within. Use a machete to cut off a section of vine with two cuts, making the high cut first. Water will then dribble out of the vine from the bottom. If this water is perfectly clear, odourless and does not burn your skin or tongue to the touch, it is safe to drink directly from the vine.

Green bamboo contains water in the hollow stems. To access it, bend down a long stalk of bamboo, tie it so that it doesn't spring

Rain trap

Tree trunk water collection

back into place, then cut off the end. Again, drink the water only if it is clear, odourless and non-caustic.

Banana or plantain trees collect water in the trunks. To access this, cut down the tree to leave a stump 30cm (12in) high, and scoop out the centre of the stump into a bowl shape. This natural bowl will fill up with water, and continue to do so for several days.

Getting water from a vine

Melting Snow

Never eat snow in its frozen state; this can result in tissue damage to the lips and throat, and accelerated hypothermia. This simple melting device consists of a cloth bag, filled with snow and fixed to a tripod near to a fire, the bag suspended over a collection container.

Water Filter

This water filter system relies on multiple layers of contrasting material, held in a water-permeable bag, to trap and hold particles held in the water. Pour the water in through the top of the filter and collect at the bottom.

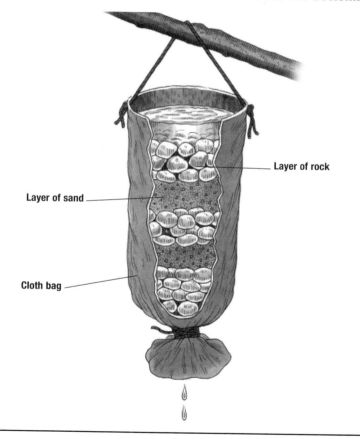

Layer of rock

Layer of sand

Cloth bag

The above advice about water collection must be taken in the context of your overall need to evade capture. Particularly in tropical or arid areas, water courses can be places that attract human activity. Carefully scan an area before going out to collect water, and try to avoid leaving tell-tale footprints in muddy river banks. If you have to collect water at night, watch out for local wildlife – predators will often hunt around waterholes during the hours of darkness.

Finding Food

One of the greatest acts of military survival was also one of the most unnecessary. During World War II, some 1000 Japanese soldiers hid out in the jungles of Guam after the US conquest of the island in 1944. Most of these men either died of starvation and disease, or were eventually captured, but one soldier, Soichi Yokio, refused to capitulate even when the war ended in 1945. Making his home in an isolated cave, he perpetuated his evasion experience until 1972. To survive he drank from rivers and other natural water sources, and lived off fruit, nuts, frogs, rats, snails, fish and shrimp. His existence came to light only when two American hunters came across him while he was fishing, and took him to a local police station. It appeared that by this time he was well aware that the war was over, but

wanted 'to live for the sake of the Emperor and believing in the Emperor and the Japanese spirit'.

The reason Soichi Yokio was able to survive for such a long time in the wilderness was that he identified a plentiful, safe diet on which he could rely. Survival nutrition is a big topic, as each environment presents a bewildering variety of plant and animal life, not all of which is safe to eat. For this reason, conduct detailed research into the flora and fauna of any region to which you are being deployed. This may seem like an unnecessarily academic exercise, given that your military catering services are likely to provide you with all the food you need, but you never know when such knowledge might become invaluable in an escape and evasion scenario.

Plant food

The world teems with plant life, so it forms one of the most accessible sources of food in the wild. The nutritional value of plant foods can be excellent. Nuts provide high amounts of fat, protein and energy; berries and leaves can supply you with most of the vitamins you need; roots make a filling, nutritious bulk food, and can also contain plenty of water.

Yet in the proliferation of plants lies the danger. The very diversity of plant species makes identification a challenge, and while some plants offer sound sustenance, others can

Tree Climbing

This method of tree climbing requires strong arms and legs, and good technique. Turn your feet sideways and push them hard into the trunk of the tree, and lean back away from the trunk as you climb.

Types of Edible Nuts

Nuts provide one of the best foods possible when attempting to survive in the wilderness. High in fat and protein, they deliver lots of energy-giving calories and they also have the advantage of being easy to transport and comparatively durable to store for long periods.

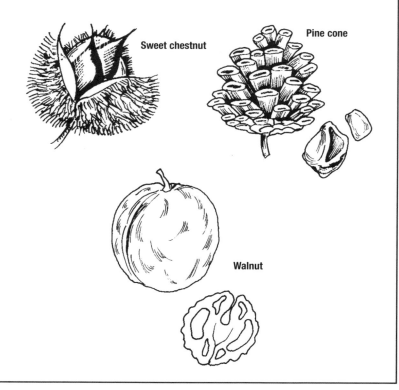

Sweet chestnut

Pine cone

Walnut

kill you with powerful toxins. Poisonous hemlock, for example, resembles wild parsnip and wild carrot, as some people have found out to their cost. Here space allows us to identify only some common plant foods by name – you must make the investment to learn what they look like with a good field guide.

Given that some plants are so dangerous, however, we can draw up some basic rules about what plants you should diligently avoid. Any plant with a milky or otherwise coloured sap is not good eating, and you should also avoid plants that give off a bitter almond-like scent – this can indicate a naturally occurring cyanide in the plant (crush up some of the leaves and woody parts to see if the smell is released).

Similarly, any plant that has an unpleasantly bitter or 'soapy' taste should be rejected. Don't eat plants that have hairs, spines or thorns on them – these can act as irritants in your mouth and throat. Official US Army survival advice also recommends avoiding 'beans, bulbs, or seeds inside pods', for the same reasons that it recommends not eating fungi – unless you can positively identify the species, you could end up ingesting something poisonous. Similarly, it states that you shouldn't consume 'grain heads with pink, purplish, or black spurs' and plants exhibiting a 'three-leaved growth pattern'. Don't rely upon observations of what animals (even primates) eat as guidance to what you can consume, as many animals can consume foodstuffs that would induce illness in a human.

These guidelines can help you to exclude many of the plants that are unsuitable for eating, and this chapter contains a useful list of common plant foods in temperate, tropical and desert regions, all of which you should learn to identify. If you are in desperate need of food, however, and you are struggling to identify the local plant life, you can always perform the Universal Edibility Test (UET). The UET is a systematic approach to testing out the edibility of a plant in a progressive and safe way. It is part of official US Army survival teaching, and is quoted below, but it must be followed exactly to be authoritative. Note also that the UET does not work with fungi – another reason to leave fungi alone unless you are something of a field expert. The UET is a sound way to identify wild food without an exhaustive botanical knowledge. Once you have found several edible plant foods, you can start to combine them into recipes that improve flavours and give your morale a boost.

Animal Food

Although some plants endure throughout winter months, seasonal variations in plant growth generally

Tip: Edible Plant Foods

The following lists show common edible plants in temperate, tropical and desert regions. Using a good field guide, ensure that you can identify these plants accurately. A positive identification is made when all elements of the plant match the description and illustration/photo, such as overall structure, height, leaves, nuts, berries, buds, colouration and flowers. Also note cooking methods – nettles, for example, require boiling before eating to kill their stinging chemicals.

Edible Temperate Zone Food Plants

Dandelion

Wild sorrel

- Amaranth (*Amaranthus retroflexus* and other species).
- Arrowroot (*Sagittaria* species).
- Asparagus (*Asparagus officinalis*).
- Beechnut (*Fagus* species).
- Blackberries (*Rubus* species).
- Blueberries (*Vaccinium* species).
- Burdock (*Arctium lappa*).
- Cattail (*Typha* species).
- Chestnut (*Castanea* species).
- Chicory (*Cichorium intybus*).
- Chufa (*Cyperus esculentus*).
- Dandelion (*Taraxacum officinale*).
- Daylily (*Hemerocallis fulva*).
- Nettle (*Urtica* species).
- Oaks (*Quercus* species).
- Persimmon (*Diospyros virginiana*).
- Plantain (*Plantago* species).

- Pokeweed (*Phytolacca americana*).
- Prickly pear cactus (*Opuntia* species).
- Purslane (*Portulaca oleracea*).
- Sassafras (*Sassafras albidum*).
- Sheep sorrel (*Rumex acetosella*).
- Strawberries (*Fragaria* species).
- Thistle (*Cirsium* species).
- Water lily and lotus (*Nuphar*, *Nelumbo*, and other species).
- Wild onion and garlic (*Allium* species).
- Wild rose (*Rosa* species).
- Wood sorrel (*Oxalis* species).

Tropical Zone Food Plants
- Bamboo (*Bambusa* and other species).
- Bananas (*Musa* species).
- Breadfruit (*Artocarpus incisa*).
- Cashew nut (*Anacardium occidental*).
- Coconut (*Cocos nucifera*).
- Mango (*Mangifera indica*).
- Palms (various species).
- Papaya (*Carica* species).
- Sugarcane (*Saccharum officinarum*).
- Taro (*Colocasia* species).

Desert Zone Food Plants
- Acacia (*Acacia farnesiana*).
- Agave (*Agave* species).
- Cactus (various species).
- Date palm (*Phoenix dactylifera*).
- Desert amaranth (*Amaranthus palmeri*).

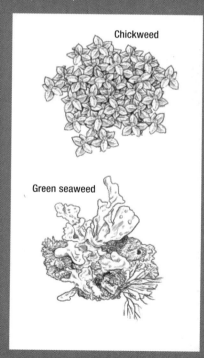

Chickweed

Green seaweed

Tip: US Army Universal Edibility Test

1. Test only one part of a potential food plant at a time.
2. Separate the plant into its basic components – leaves, stems, roots, buds, and flowers.
3. Smell the food for strong or acid odours. Remember, smell alone does not indicate a plant is edible or inedible.
4. Do not eat for 8 hours before starting the test.
5. During the 8 hours you abstain from eating, test for contact poisoning by placing a piece of the plant part you are testing on the inside of your elbow or wrist. Usually 15 minutes is enough time to allow for a reaction.
6. During the test period, take nothing by mouth except purified water and the plant part you are testing.
7. Select a small portion of a single part and prepare it the way you plan to eat it.
8. Before placing the prepared plant part in your mouth, touch a small portion (a pinch) to the outer surface of your lip to test for burning or itching.

mean that animals are a necessary survival food. Meat provides protein and energy in good measures, but has the obvious disadvantage that it has to be caught before it can be consumed. Catching an animal is no easy matter. Animals live in a world of constant danger and have developed superior senses to detect threats. In a peacetime hunting scenario, those senses are often overcome by humans through the use of firearms, but in an evasion situation a gunshot splitting the silence of the wilderness is an auditory beacon to your location. For these reasons, you'll probably have to fall back on far older methods of hunting.

The animals that you hunt naturally vary according to your location in the world. Mammals, fish and birds are the most profitable to kill, as they provide an appropriate payoff for the energy expended while hunting, in terms of the volume

9. If after 3 minutes there is no reaction on your lip, place the plant part on your tongue, holding it there for 15 minutes.
10. If there is no reaction, thoroughly chew a pinch and hold it in your mouth for 15 minutes. Do not swallow.
11. If no burning, itching, numbing, stinging, or other irritation occurs during the 15 minutes, swallow the food.
12. Wait 8 hours. If any ill effects occur during this period, induce vomiting and drink a lot of water.
13. If no ill effects occur, eat 0.25 cup of the same plant part prepared the same way. Wait another 8 hours. If no ill effects occur, the plant part as prepared is safe for eating.

CAUTION

Test all parts of the plant for edibility, as some plants have both edible and inedible parts. Do not assume that a part that proved edible when cooked is also edible when raw. Test the part raw to ensure edibility before eating raw. The same part or plant may produce varying reactions in different individuals.

of meat obtained. Classic wild animal foods include rabbits, hares, wild dogs, wild sheep, deer, antelope, wild goats, pigs and squirrels, but the needs of survival widen the remit into the unpalatable world of insects, grubs and various amphibians and reptiles.

One important point, however, is that you should attempt to hunt and kill only those animals you can confidently handle, to avoid the risk of injury from a creature literally fighting for its life. You need to make some weapons, therefore, and examples of these are listed below. These require some basic engineering. If you don't have a knife, you can fashion one from a tin can lid or similar piece of metal; a rock with a sharp, splintered edge; or a piece of robust glass attached to a handle. Whatever you produce, it needs to be sharp enough to take shavings off wood, and to penetrate a thick animal hide.

Hunting weapons
Club
A hefty wooden club can be used to kill even large mammals such as sheep and goats. Make such a weapon from a branch about 5–6cm (2–2.5in) in diameter, preferably widening towards the striking end, and about 75cm (2ft 6in) long.

Spear
A throwing spear should be about 90cm (35in) long, and a stabbing spear up to 180cm (6ft) long. Hold the carved point over a fire to harden it. You can make more durable and lethal points by splitting the shaft at the end and inserting a piece of sharp metal or bone into the split before lashing it securely in place.

Throwing stick
Throwing sticks are practical weapons for bringing down rabbits, squirrels, birds and other small creatures. The best sticks will be

Throwing Spear

Here we see a hunter about to attack his prey using a spear and spear-thrower. The spear-throwing device is whipped forward to increase the acceleration of the spear through leverage. With practice, a survivor could hit prey at up to 100m (328ft).

slightly bent in shape, although a straight stick about 60cm (24in) long with a thickened end is perfectly useable. Skim the stick on a horizontal plane to maximize the chances of hitting the target. Don't make the throwing stick too heavy, otherwise you won't be able to throw it very far or with the speed required to deliver a stunning blow.

Stones

Stones are the most immediate of weapons. One of their most practical applications is for delivering the *coup de grace* to an injured animal, simply by using a heavy rock to strike it on the head. With a little skill on your part, many small animals can be killed by thrown stones, as long as the stones are smooth (smooth stones fly better), have enough weight to stun and will fit easily in the hand. When trying to hit birds, try throwing several stones at once in a 'shotgun' effect.

Types of Spearhead

Spearheads can be modified for different purposes. The two spearheads on the left here would ideally be suited to spear fishing, while the two on the right are more practical for delivering deep penetration into large mammals.

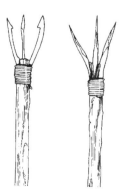

Catapult

A catapult is highly accurate in practised hands, and will easily kill small mammals and birds at a range of 10m (32ft) and beyond. The simplest catapult consists of little more than a forked twig with a piece of elastic material fitted between the forks, and a pouch of material fitted onto the elastic to hold the projectile. The elastic from clothes will work reasonably, but it is far better to use high-quality elastics such as surgical tubing or even rubber cut from a tyre inner tube. When shooting with a catapult, grip the shaft horizontally so that the open mouth of the forks points to one side; this way you can use the uppermost fork as a rudimentary sight.

Slingshot

Slingshots are an ancient hunting weapon, but they take considerable practice to master. You can make a slingshot with a length of string or cord about 1.37m (4ft) long, with a patch of leather or cloth in the centre. To use the slingshot, place a stone securely in the patch, hold both ends of the cord and swing the sling around in a fast circle above your head. As the projectile whips towards the target, let go of one end of the cord to project the stone.

Bola

The bola is used to kill flying birds or bring down running animals. It delivers its effect in two ways: its multiple cords entangle an animal and stop it running or flying, while the weights at the end of the cords deliver a simultaneous impact to stun or kill the creature. To make a bola, wrap three to six stones, each about 5cm (2in) in diameter, in individual pouches of material, then tie each pouch to a piece of string about 1m (3ft) long. Gather all the ends of the strings and knot them together very firmly. Launch the bola by holding the knotted ends and swinging the whole device above your head for several revolutions before throwing it at your prey. A good bola is powerful enough to kill quite substantial animals, and for this reason take care that you do not strike yourself while swinging it around your head.

Bow and arrow

A well-made bow and arrow will kill large prey such as deer and goats at distances of up to 100m (328ft). In an emergency, when time is short, you can construct a bow from green, unseasoned wood. Although this bow won't have the power or durability of one made from properly seasoned wood, it will still suffice for the short term.

To make a bow, choose a flexible, strong wood such as yew, willow, locust, cedar, hickory, ash, oak, elm, birch or maple. The bow should be about 120cm (4ft) long, carved so that it is evenly weighted at both

Sling

The sling is an ancient weapon that can bring down small animals if used with accuracy and force. The one downside for the escapee is that the sling requires considerable practice to master – practice that is unlikely to be acquired while on the run.

ends and widens in the centre (but not more than 5cm/2in) to form a handgrip, wrapped tightly in strips of leather or cloth. Cut notches about 1.25cm (0.5in) from the bow tips to hold a string made from rawhide or any other durable cord. Sling the bow securely, but do not put it under too much tension or the bow will have limited pull and reduced range. Rub the bow with animal fat or oil to prevent the wood from drying out.

Fashion arrows from hardwood shafts about 60cm (2ft) long and

6mm (0.25in) wide, with any irregularities on the surface of the wood smoothed out. You can straighten crooked shafts by warming them over hot rocks, then allowing the shafts to cool while holding them in a straight position. Simply sharpening the wood forms a point, though better penetration will be achieved by attaching pointed pieces of stone, bone, metal or glass. Use feathers, paper, cloth or even leaves to make flights – three equally spaced flights are optimum – and notch the blunt end of the arrow to fit into the bowstring.

When shooting a bow, keep the arm gripping the bow locked as you pull the bowstring back with your other hand. Pull the bowstring back

Bola

The bola missile works in two ways. When striking an animal, the cords tangle its legs and help to bring it down, while the weights at the end of each cord act as impact points to stun or kill the creature.

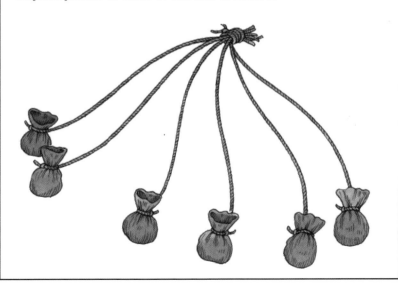

Making a Bow

A bow is an excellent hunting and fighting weapon, although it may well take several attempts to create a reasonably efficient design. Use strong cord for the bowstring, as it will have to endure extreme pressure when it is pulled for firing.

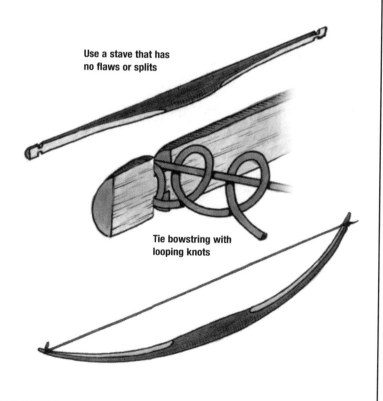

Use a stave that has no flaws or splits

Tie bowstring with looping knots

to the side of your face, but be careful the string doesn't get hooked behind your ear. Line up the target with the arrow and release the string with a natural unfurling of the fingers.

Active Hunting

Hunting down animals using the weapons described above takes skill and patience. In an evasion situation this is doubly difficult, as you have to stay aware of human threats while stalking your prey. Your essential objective is to approach the target animal to a distance at which you can then deploy your weapon effectively. First, of course, you have to find the animal. Look for evidence of animal presence in the form of footprints, droppings, chewed vegetation, animal remains (indicating the presence of a carnivore) and noises. Many animals are territorial, and they will often use certain tracks

Smoking out your Prey

One way to flush out a rabbit or similar burrow-dwelling creature is to light a fire near the hole, waft smoke down into the burrow, and club the animal when it emerges, trying to escape from the fumes.

and watering holes regularly, which you can stake out nearby.

When you are stalking a creature, stay downwind and use all available natural cover to mask your movements as you approach. Don't silhouette yourself at any point, and apply the same camouflage principles outlined in Chapter 1 (see especially pages 44–45). Remember that when you get within striking distance, you must attack with purpose to kill the animal. Larger animals, such as deer, will often run away wounded if hit with a spear or arrow. Don't immediately sprint after the creature – this will encourage the wounded animal to keep going, and will also put you in danger of being spotted. Instead, wait a few minutes and then begin carefully tracking the blood trail. Eventually you should come across the dead or collapsed animal.

Snare traps

Hunting is a difficult and uncertain business. Even experienced hunters armed with modern hunting rifles or

Snare Wire

The great value of the snare as a hunting device is its simplicity and reliability. Much of the knack of using a snare successfully comes from its placement rather than its functionality.

Squirrel Snare

Squirrels tend to use predictable routes through the trees within their territories. Place small snare loops at several locations along key branches, and you stand a good chance of catching a squirrel as it scampers across the branch.

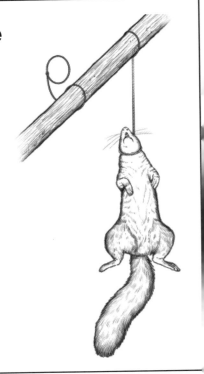

shotguns often return from the field empty-handed. To maximize your chances of catching animals, traps and snares offer the advantage of working even while you are absent, and by setting multiple traps you can effectively be 'hunting' in several different locations at once.

The three basic types of trap are snares, spear traps and deadfall traps. Snares will be explained in detail below, but deadfall traps (killing via the triggered drop of a heavy weight) and spear traps (traps that release spikes under tension) will not, despite the fact that they feature in most survival manuals. Both of these types of trap take substantial time to construct – time that generally isn't available to you in an evasion situation. Having just escaped from a POW camp, you are likely to be moving fast through the terrain, and often laying up during the day. A snare trap can be rigged up in minutes and taken down just as easily, whereas some of the larger traps require sharpened stakes and elaborate trigger mechanisms, plus are often more visible to searching eyes than a small snare hidden discretely in a bush. It is still recommended that you look into how to make these traps, to hone your overall survival skills, but in the context of a fast-moving evasion situation they have limited application.

At their most basic, snares consist of a looped wire, the loop free-running by virtue of a slip-knot. The end of the wire is secured to a solid object and the loop is positioned in a location along which an animal is likely to pass. Should the animal put its leg, head or body into the loop, the loop will pull tight around the animal as it moves away and then struggles to free itself. The snare will then hold the animal until you revisit the trap, to find the animal either dead from strangulation or at least trapped for you to kill.

An improvement on a basic snare involves using a 'twitch-up' branch. Here the end of the wire is tied to a hooked peg, which lightly engages a similarly hooked stake embedded in the ground. The peg is held under

Tip: 'Channelizing' Traps

Traps or snares placed on a trail or run should use channelization. To build a channel, construct a funnel-shaped barrier extending from the sides of the trail toward the trap, with the narrowest part nearest the trap. Channelization should be inconspicuous to avoid alerting the prey. As the animal gets to the trap, it cannot turn left or right and continues into the trap. Few wild animals will back up, preferring to face the direction of travel. Channelization does not have to be an impassable barrier. You only have to make it inconvenient for the animal to go over or through the barrier. For best effect, the channelization should reduce the trail's width to just slightly wider than the targeted animal's body. Maintain this constriction at least as far back from the trap as the animal's body length, then begin the widening toward the mouth of the funnel.
– Field Manual 21-76, *US Army Survival Manual*

'Channelized' Snare

This snare wire loop has been placed at the end of a channel of vegetation. The channel controls the route of travel of an animal, which will hopefully walk straight into the loop and be trapped.

Killing a Rabbit

An age-old way of dispatching a rabbit involves picking it up by its back legs and chopping hard on the back of its neck with the edge of the hand. This technique is best delivered when the rabbit is already stunned or injured, as a fully alert rabbit will struggle ferociously.

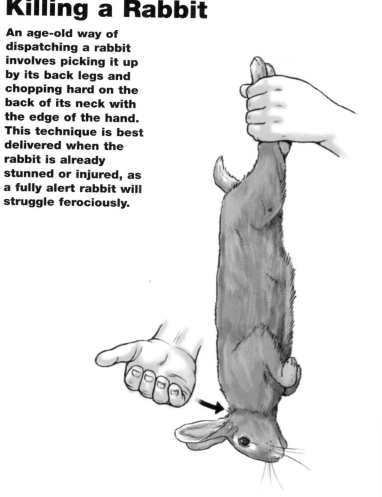

Spring Snare

This spring snare utilizes a bent branch to provide tension and a wooden notched trigger system to hold the snare loop in place on the ground. When the trigger disengages, caused by an animal getting caught in the loop, the branch tension is released, whipping the animal into the air.

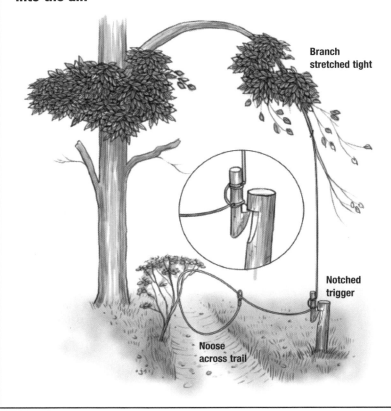

Branch stretched tight

Notched trigger

Noose across trail

tension by a cord tied between it and a bent-over sapling or branch. When an animal is caught by the snare loop and pulls on the wire, the 'trigger' system is unlocked; the animal is then lifted into the air as the bent branch is released. The advantage of this system is that the catch is held away from predators, which are just as interested in the kill as you are, and it prevents the animal being able to struggle free as easily as it would on the ground.

Effective use of snares depends on several factors other than mere construction. Limit your handling of the trap to keep your smell off it; rubbing your hands in mud before making the trap is one way to limit scent transfer. You can also use the principle of 'channelization' to guide the animal into the snare, or indeed other trap (see feature box, page 183). The trap can be made more tempting by scattering around the mouth of the snare some bait (such as scraps of meat or nuts) that is appropriate to your prey type.

Fishing

Fishing is an ideal method of acquiring meat, but for reasons touched on above carries risks in a survival situation. Waterways are frequently the site of human habitation or a route of human traffic, so spending time by the water's edge fishing naturally carries risk to an escaped prisoner. Try to fish in parts of the river where you can conceal yourself on the bank. Fishing during low-light conditions under overhanging foliage, for example, will make you hard to spot. Stay vigilant for the sounds of boat traffic or for human voices moving along the river bank – human trails often wind their way alongside rivers.

The most accessible method of survival fishing simply involves using a hook and line. Ideally, if you have a professional survival tin with you, it will contain proper line, hooks and weights. If you don't have such items, they can be crafted from natural materials. Sharp thorns, bent pins or nails, or slim pieces of bone or wood can be fashioned into hooks, while pieces of strong cotton or string, or even lengths of long grass, can become line. Feathers will act as lures; pieces of wood or cork as floats; small stones as weights. A basic fishing rod can be nothing more than a long, flexible stick. Use your imagination and creativity, but also understand how to read a river to improve the results of your fishing.

Fish often enjoy the cover of river banks or other shaded spots, particularly if the weather is hot, while in cold weather they tend to move towards sunnier patches of water to get warm. Indicators of fish include ring ripples punctuating the water's surface. The refraction of light through water means that the fish will have a good view over the edge of

Fishing Locations

Fish can often be found in places where the current slows, or where the shade provided by logs, rocks or overhanging vegetation gives the fish shade from the sun (if the weather is hot) or protection from predators.

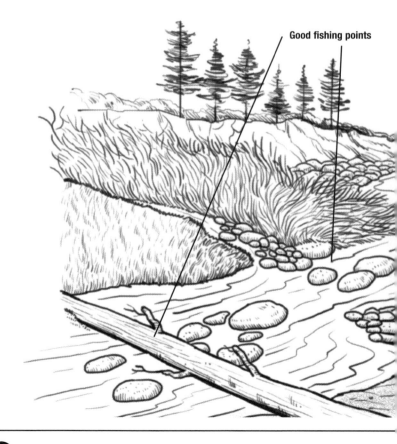

Good fishing points

Good fishing point

the bank, so stay low down to avoid scaring the fish away.

Note that you don't actually need to be present at the riverside to perform traditional hook and line fishing. You can fix the line to a stick embedded into the bank, and leave it for some time in the water before returning to check it. Alternatively, you could tie a piece of cord between two sticks, one on each side of a narrow section of stream, and then have multiple lines draped down into the water. Using a fishing device such as this, you can maximize your chances of a decent catch, but you should check the lines regularly so that predatory fish do not take your dinner. Refuse can also be used to trap fish. If you come across an empty plastic drinks bottle, cut off the top third of the bottle and fit this portion in a reverse direction back into the bottle body. Also put some bait, such as worms or insects, into the bottom. Then submerge what is now a basic fish trap – a fish can easily swim into the bottle through the inverted neck, but it will struggle to get out in the reverse direction.

Fish traps

A similar principle can be applied to fashioning fish traps from rocks and wooden stakes. In coastal regions, for example, you could build a semi-circular fish corral against the shoreline at high tide; at low tide the water level will drop, leaving any fish

Making a Spiked Harpoon

To make a spiked harpoon, cut a series of notches in the end of a long shaft of wood, and bind strong, sharp thorns into these notches with cord. You can insert a small piece of wood between the thorns to make them splay out and therefore increase the striking area.

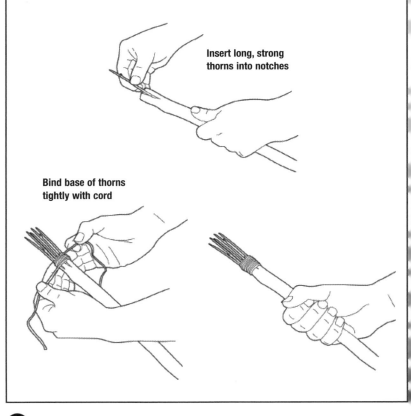

Insert long, strong thorns into notches

Bind base of thorns tightly with cord

Corralling Fish

In this simple fish trap, the survivor uses sticks to create a small entrance passage into a corral. The stream's current should flow directly into the trap to help guide the fish through the entrance.

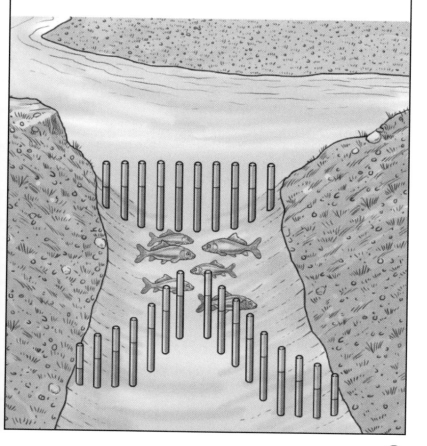

Tip: Food from the Coastline

Coastlines are excellent places from which to gather wild foods. They include the following:

- Seaweed – high in vitamin C and essential minerals, seaweed is an easily gathered food from shorelines. Tough seaweeds can be dried and cooked over a fire until brittle or boiled, although soft varieties can be eaten raw.
- Mussels – Remove any sand, grit and the mussel's beard. Discard any that are open and which do not close when tapped. Cook before eating, throwing away any that stay closed after the cooking process. (Learn to identify and avoid the northern black mussel, which can contain severe toxins, and in the tropics don't eat mussels during the summer months.)
- Crabs and shellfish – Many different types of shellfish often reveal themselves in rocky pools at low tide, or are washed onto beaches after stormy weather. However, never eat any shellfish that are not covered by the water at high tide.

in the corral stranded inside. Such large constructions, however, might well be beyond your time, means and energy during an evasion action. A more rough and ready option, therefore, is spear fishing. You can make a basic fish spear from a long shaft of wood, to which you bind multiple long thorns or sharpened spikes of wood or bone at one end. (Splay these impact points outwards, to broaden the striking surface.) Alternatively, you could always tie your survival knife to the end of the shaft, but make sure the binding is very firm,

as you don't want your precious knife to disappear into the river.

To hunt fish by spear, squat on the bank or stand in the shallows of the water. Keep very still, and allow fish to swim around you. Place the tip of the spear gently in the water, and wait until a fish approaches to striking distance. As soon as one is in range, thrust the spear down sharply, skewering the fish to the bottom of the riverbed. Keep the spear in place, and reach down with your spare hand and grip the fish firmly, before lifting your kill out onto the river bank.

Insects

Insects are a valuable source of survival food, however unpleasant that prospect might seem. They provide fats, carbohydrates and proteins, and many can be eaten raw, meaning that you can avoid the need to make a fire. Never eat insects that are found on dung, carrion or refuse, however, because they may well be carrying diseases – this means avoiding flies, mosquitoes and ticks. Similarly, you should avoid insects with extremely bright colours or extravagant patterns – these are often nature's warning signs that a creature is poisonous. Also stay away from anything hairy, as such hairs often hold irritant chemicals.

The list of edible insects is huge, but many require positive identification. A 'safe' list, however, is worms, beetle grubs, locusts, grasshoppers, crickets and beetles.

- Worms – After collecting, starve them for 24 hours and then squeeze out their innards between thumb and forefinger.
- Beetle larvae – Look for these in rotting logs. They can be eaten raw, but they are far more pleasant to consume if cooked.
- Locusts, grasshoppers, crickets, beetles – These can be caught by swatting them with a branch. Remove the legs, head and wings before eating, and ideally cook by roasting.

Food from human sources

Having cautioned about avoiding people, one other way to obtain food is simply to steal it from locals. Sometimes this could involve taking foods growing on farmland, but it could also mean more high-risk theft. Keep isolated buildings under observation, noting who lives in the house and when they come and go. If you are confident that the premises are empty, then you can explore for sources of food and drink, while also watching for remaining four-legged members of the family in the form of guard dogs. Look also for outlying wells or water butts, to provide you with drinking water.

The dangers of stealing food from local people are evident in the epic escape story of Dieter Dengler, a US Navy Skyraider pilot during the Vietnam War who was shot down over Laos on 1 February 1966. He was incarcerated alongside six other prisoners, including two Americans, Duane W. Martin and Eugene De Bruin, in a brutal Laotian POW camp, where they were mistreated and virtually starved. From the outset Dengler set his mind on escape, and he hatched a plan that involved the POWs breaking out of their hut while the guards were eating, stealing the guards' weapons and taking over the camp. The breakout was executed on 29 June 1966, and was successful, although Dengler was forced to kill three guards with an AK-47. Now on

Termites as Food

Termites are actually a good source of survival food, being high in fat and protein and relatively easy to catch. They can be acquired by pushing a long stick into a termite nest; the termites will attack the stick and will cling to it as it is withdrawn from the nest.

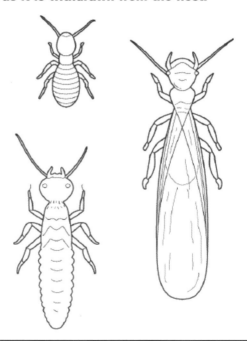

the run in the hostile Laotian jungle, the men split up, Dengler going with Duane Martin, another American pilot. Despite having a little food with them (some rice taken from the camp), both men were suffering from the effects of starvation. Martin also had malaria. They decided, against Dengler's better judgement, to try to obtain food from a remote native village, but as they approached the village they were confronted by a hostile civilian armed with a machete. In a horrifying moment, the civilian swung the machete into Martin's neck, killing him instantly. Dengler managed to avoid being attacked himself, but the incident was a terrible illustration of how everyone can be a potential threat in an evasion wilderness.

We will return to Dengler's experience in this chapter, and later chapters. Of course, there have been many instances of locals actively helping soldiers to evade capture, even providing temporary accommodation. In these cases, you must never stay too long, however. Prolonged stays increase the danger of discovery, particularly as other, less sympathetic locals might become suspicious of changes in the behaviour and movements of their neighbour. Remember that although you are on the run, you also owe it to

Agricultural Sources

Agricultural land can obviously be an easy place to acquire fruit and vegetables. Try not to expose yourself in the middle of a field, however; stay low and take food from the edges of the field.

Sod Fire and Reflector

Here a fire is built in a trench made simply by cutting and folding back the top layer of earth. Note also the basic reflector in the background, made from logs and rocks – if the person sits between the fire and the reflector, his back will be warmed as well as his front.

any helpers not to put them in unnecessary jeopardy.

Fire

The ability to make fire is invaluable in a survival situation. A good camp fire will provide you with heat – possibly life-saving heat in winter conditions – plus the means to cook food and boil water. The problem in escape and evasion situations is naturally that a fire can, by its light

and smoke, give away your location to a pursuing enemy. Ultimately, the risks must be weighed against each other. If a fire is all that stands between you and freezing to death, then make a fire. You can limit the visibility of a fire by building it under trees that form a dense canopy of foliage, which will disperse the smoke and hide the flames. Fires made at dusk and dawn are less likely to attract attention than those made in pitch blackness. US armed forces advice also recommends timing the making of a fire to the hours when locals light their own fires for cooking.

Four elements have to be present in any fire: tinder, kindling, fuel and oxygen. Tinder consists of any very light, absolutely dry material that ignites easily under spark or heat, and which provides your first flames.

Good examples of tinders are dry grasses (rub them in your hands to open up the fibres), pieces of lint or cotton wool, dry mosses, wood shavings and the inside of birds' nests. Once the tinder is lit, you need to build up the heat of the fire by adding kindling. Kindling is typically light, dry sticks that catch fire easily over the incipient flame. Once the fire is established, you can then add the

Teepee Fire

A teepee fire ignites quickly and burns with a lot of heat and light, and little smoke (if you use the right wood). When the fire collapses, you can add heavier fuel to control the rate of burn.

fuel of more substantial logs, to bring the fire to full heat. At every stage of the fire-building process, the fire needs to be open to the air, as flames require oxygen to burn.

You can subsequently alter the intensity of a fire by either increasing or decreasing its access to the air supply.

Making fire

There are numerous ways to make fire if you don't have matches or a lighter, but some are more labour-intensive than others. The most advanced methods are the fire drill and fire plough. Both rely on generating a flame through the heat of friction. A fire drill consists of two basic components: a flat hardwood baseboard and a softwood spindle about 30–40cm (12–18in) long and about 2cm (0.75in) in diameter, sharpened into a blunt point at one end. Cut a V-shaped notch into the edge of the baseboard, plus a circular indentation at the top of the 'V'. To use the fire drill, place a handful of tinder beneath the notch, then insert the pointed end of the spindle into the baseboard's indentation. Now start rubbing the spindle between your hands in a repetitive circular downward motion (as if rubbing your hands together to get warm), causing the spindle to rotate in the hole on the baseboard. Friction between the spindle and board eventually generates hot flakes

of wood, which can be pushed onto the tinder and will cause it to ignite (blow gently on the tinder to encourage the flames). The fire drill, however, when operated purely by the rubbing method, is a long and exhausting method of making fire. It can be speeded up by making a bow to accelerate the rotations of the drill – see the illustration on page 200 for how this can be done.

The fire plough works along the same lines as the fire drill. The main difference is that the baseplate now features a long groove, along which a stick is rubbed back and forth vigorously until a hot coal is created and pushed off the end of the baseplate onto tinder.

In the tropics, a variation of the fire plough is the bamboo saw. Take a section of bamboo about 50cm (20in) long and split it lengthwise (you need a sharp knife to make the bamboo saw). Scrape your knife along the outside of one half of the bamboo (let's call this Section 1) – the shavings will make excellent tinder. Now take the other half (Section 2) and cut a notch in it half-way along, almost through to the inside. Place the tinder inside Section 1, positioned over the notch and held in place by two splints of wood, gripped by your hands. Kneel on the floor and wedge Section 1 between the floor and your stomach, with the inside of the bamboo facing upwards. Then take Section 2 and place it at a right angle to Section 1, with the notch running along one edge of Section 1. Now start rubbing Section 2 vigorously backwards and forwards. Eventually, the build-up of heat in the notch creates a coal directly beneath the tinder, and gentle blowing can produce a flame.

These advanced forms of firelighting take practice to perfect. They can be especially stubborn in damp conditions, or if you are in a weakened condition. Dieter Dengler, for example, attempted the bamboo saw method of firelighting during his evasion in Laos, but his state of near-starvation meant that he was unable to raise a flame. He solved the problem, however, by emptying out some carbine cartridges and using the propellant inside to elicit a fire. Other convenient methods of fire-starting are listed in the feature box on page 202.

Fire Plough

The fire plough is an exhausting method of lighting a fire, but one that can still work with the right materials and persistence. Maintain a strong, constant pressure on the stick running along the groove, and use strokes about 10–20cm (4–8in) long.

Bow Drill

The bow drill is one of the more advanced methods of survival firelighting. Time spent making each component correctly will produce better final results, although in damp weather this technique remains unpredictable.

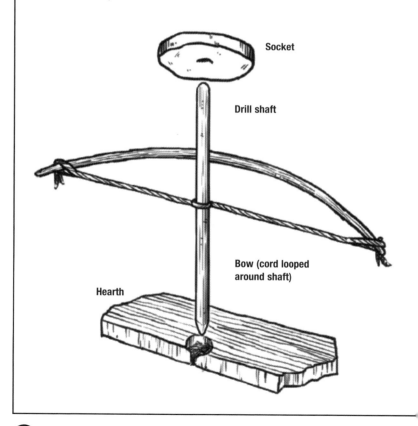

Socket

Drill shaft

Bow (cord looped around shaft)

Hearth

Maintain pressure on the hand socket and move the bow drill smoothly and quickly.

Blow gently on the tinder as it begins to smoulder.

Cooking Fires

Almost any type of hot fire can be used for cooking (cooler, smoky fires are suitable for food-preservation techniques). For example, a trench fire can be used as a grill by making a wire mesh or a grid of green sticks over the trench on which to place food. (You must use green sticks; mature wood will catch alight.) Make sure that any fire is up to temperature before starting to cook. The hottest point is usually when large flames die down and the wood forms itself into hot coals.

Don't position food too close to a fire, as it may simply char on the outside while remaining uncooked on the inside. You can check whether meat is properly cooked by driving a knife or wooden skewer into the middle of the meat and withdrawing it. If the juices run out red, it is not yet cooked. If they run clear, the food is OK to eat. Also, tentatively touch the end of a skewer. If it is hot, that means the central part of the food has been cooking.

Yukon Stove

A Yukon Stove is an effective way to create a cooking fire (see instructions opposite). When fire is started in the Yukon stove, it produces considerable heat; feed it with sticks, either through the channel or simply by dropping them down the funnel.

The heat is controlled by limiting the influx of oxygen by partially closing the vent at the top. Place food on skewers or a grill, and position them over the vent to cook. Alternatively, wrap food in parcels of leaves and put them just inside the fire channel.

Tip: Fire-starting Methods

Lens – On sunny days, capture and direct sunlight into a point on tinder, blowing gently to encourage a flame.

Flint and steel – Striking a piece of steel against flint can produce sufficient sparks to ignite tinder. Commercially produced fire strikers produce by far the best results, however. They sometimes feature magnesium blocks – shave off strips of magnesium into your tinder for near instant ignition.

Battery – Place two pieces of wire on the opposing terminals of a battery. Bring the ends of the wire together in a pile of tinder to create sparks and a flame.

Yukon Stove

Dig a circular hole in the ground about 24cm (9in) across and about 30cm (1ft) deep. Then dig a channel leading down into the hole, which will be the point for starting and feeding the fire. Next, stack up rocks around the edge of the hole in a funnel shape without closing the fire channel. If possible, try to make the funnel narrow towards the middle and flare out slightly at the top. Finally, pack the funnel with clay and earth to seal it and stabilize it.

Mud oven

First find a metal can or other vessel to act as a fireproof pot. Dig a narrow trench, and jam the pot on its side across the gap, with a space underneath for a fire. Jam a long, thick stick upright into the ground at the base of the pot and cover the body, not the mouth, of the pot with a heavy layer of earth or clay, leaving the long stick protruding. Remove this stick to create a chimney. Build a fire under the pot in the trench. The interior of the pot will become hot enough for roasting or baking foods. Hold the lid on the pot by using a forked stick.

Cooking on hot rocks

Hot rocks will provide a cooking surface for some time after flames have died down. Remember to clean off ash and pieces of burnt wood using a 'brush' made of green sticks

Preparing a Mud Oven

The mud oven is constructed by building a bank of earth over a large metal pot, using a stick to make a chimney. When constructing a mud oven, remember to leave a gap beneath the pot in which to make the fire. The mud oven is excellent for slow roasting joints of meat.

A

before laying the meat directly onto the rocks. Rock-cooking is suitable for fairly small fish and thin slices of meat.

Food preservation

If you do manage to obtain more food than you can immediately eat, try to preserve the remainder for later. Food preserving has several different functions. It delays the process of decomposition and retards the growth of germs and micro-organisms. It also helps you to conserve valuable energy by reducing time spent hunting or foraging.

Tips for Cooking and Preserving

- Catch all fats dripping from meat during cooking.
- Instead of rehydrating dried foods, grind them up into a powder and add this to soups

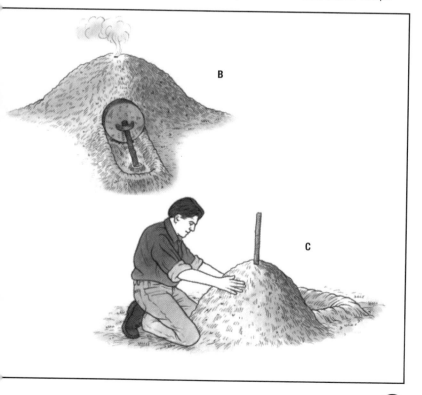

or other meals as a nutritional flavouring.

- Boil fruits to make a jelly when it cools and settles. This jelly will store for several weeks.
- Preserve fish by making pemmican. Mix flaked dried fish mixed with an equal amount of animal fat, then seal the food in a bag. Pemmican is nutritious (it contains every vitamin and mineral except vitamin C) and can remain edible, in colder climates, for more than a year.

Improvised Shelter

Sometimes shelter presents itself obviously. The interior of this downed aircraft provides decent shelter, but only if the enemy are distant and unlikely to discover the aircraft's location. An aircraft might also contain useful survival kit, such as blankets, food and fuel (for fires).

- Preserve fish or meat by salting. Smear the food with salt or, even better, store the food within layers of salt. Salting draws moisture out of the food, thus making it less habitable to bacteria that could spoil it.

Shelter

For the soldier attempting to evade pursuers, a shelter should both protect him from the elements and camouflage him from the enemy. This balance is easier said than done. Building a shelter means modifying

Lean-to Shelters

A fallen tree is often an ideal foundation for a survival shelter. By propping up thick branches against the trunk, you can create a snug survival space beneath, particularly once it is lined with a carpet of thick vegetation. You can improve the wind resistance of this shelter by packing the gaps between the logs with thick mud.

US Army Tip: Selecting a Shelter Site

The US armed services *Survival, Evasion, and Recovery* manual lists the following principles for selecting a shelter site:

When you are in a survival situation and realize that shelter is a high priority, start looking for shelter as soon as possible. As you do so, remember what you will need at the site. Two requisites are –
- It must contain material to make the type of shelter you need.
- It must be large enough and level enough for you to lie down comfortably.

When you consider these requisites, however, you cannot ignore your tactical situation or your safety. You must also consider whether the site –
- Provides concealment from enemy observation.
- Has camouflaged escape routes.
- Is suitable for signaling, if necessary.
- Provides protection against wild animals and rocks and dead trees that might fall.
- Is free from insects, reptiles, and poisonous plants.

the terrain, which can in turn increase your visibility to vigilant pursuers. Yet from a survival point of view it is imperative that you stay warm and dry, and a good shelter will give you somewhere to recuperate mentally and physically.

The points about camouflage and concealment are especially important. Build your shelters in places hidden from easy view – wooded ravines, dense forests, within

rugged, rocky terrain, etc. – but avo trapping yourself in locations with n escape routes.

A cave, for example, might give excellent shelter from the elements, but there is likely to be only one way in and out, and caves would be obvious places for enemy search parties to explore. You should have several escape routes planned for if you hear or see people approachin routes that utilize the advantages of 'dead ground' explained in Chapter 1 (see pages 48–52).

There are many types of shelter, but we start with the basic and therefore most useful varieties, particularly suitable for temperate zones. If you have a poncho, parachute, plastic sheet or tarpaulin, and a length of rope, you can create a rudimentary shelter by tying the rope between two trees and fitting the sheet over the rope in a tent-like fashion, fastening down the corners with wooden pegs. With poles, some cordage and waterproof fabrics you can build all manner of shelters, from simple lean-tos to tepee-like structures.

If you don't have these materials, then the classic survival shelter is the A-frame shelter. To make this, you take a long, straight tree bow, longer than you are tall, and prop one end in the fork of a tree a few feet off the ground. Then build up numerous other branches at an angle of 45° against the main support branch, naturally interlocking them together to form a robust, thick outer wall. Include lots of leafy material for waterproofing.

You can even 'carpet' the outside of the vegetation-covered frame with grassy sods of earth, to provide further insulation and protection. As with all shelters, make a carpet of soft foliage on the floor to sleep on (never sleep directly on the floor).

Note that you can adapt naturally occurring features in your shelters.

For example, the trunk of a fallen tree can act as one 'wall' of a lean-to shelter, or the low-hanging branches of a pine tree can provide a snow-proof roof.

A hollow in the ground can be enclosed over with branches. In certain climates and terrains, however, shelters have to be adapted to meet extreme demands.

Desert shelters

The obvious priority of a desert shelter is to protect you from scorching daytime temperatures. Seek out areas with good shading, such as rocky outcrops. If you have a sheet of fabric, then you can construct a basic shelter by stretching the material between the top of rocks or small sand dunes, securing the fabric in place with more rocks and sand. If you have enough fabric, fold this into a double-layer roof with a 30–45cm (12–18in) airspace between the layers (you can use rocks as spacers). The airspace actually acts as an insulator from the sun's heat.

To build an even cooler shelter, dig a trench about 45cm (18in) beneath the ground surface, long enough for you to lie in, and then construct the fabric roof above this trench. The combination of features could produce a shelter temperature up to half that outside, plus this shelter has the advantage of a low profile to aid concealment.

Tropical shelters

Jungles are typically very hostile at ground level, teeming with biting wildlife. For this reason, tropical shelters should be built off the ground, either in the form of wooden platforms or at least as hammocks strung between trees. You can construct a basic platform shelter by tying long sections of bamboo or other strong wooden poles between adjacent trees to form an outer framework, then laying and tying other poles across the framework to form a sleeping platform. Stringing a tarpaulin or other waterproof sheet above the platform will then provide protection from insects dropping from the trees, and also from the rainfall typical of the tropics.

Tropical regions provide plentiful materials for shelter and camp construction, and it pays to think innovatively. Split bamboo sections can be interlocked to form solid roofs with natural guttering; elephant grass and other large leaves can be woven into wooden frameworks to produce waterproof shelter; vines provide instant, tough cordage.

Arctic shelters

In sub-zero conditions, shelter is an absolute priority. Failure to find adequate shelter against the wind, rain and freezing air temperatures can mean hypothermia setting in within minutes.

The essential arctic shelter is the snow cave. As its name suggests, the snow cave is literally a dug-out that is cut into a deep snowdrift. The snow should be hard enough for you to cut a relatively narrow entrance, but widen the excavation out into a chamber large enough for you to sit up and lie down comfortably. Make a sleeping

Dinghy and Tarpaulin Shelter

Don't be afraid to improvise when making a shelter. Here a dingy and a tarpaulin are configured into a cool shelter, the structure held in place by cords and rock weights.

platform at the back of the chamber, on a level higher than the main floor of the chamber.

The extra height means that while you are sleeping (which is a time when your body temperature naturally drops) the coldest air in the cave will sink down to the lowest point, away from the platform. (Line the sleeping platform with pine branches to provide an insulating material – never sleep directly on the snow.)

You can block up the entrance, once you are inside, with a compact ball of snow or any other material to hand, but make sure that your snow cave features at least one ventilation hole bored right through the wall of the cave, otherwise you

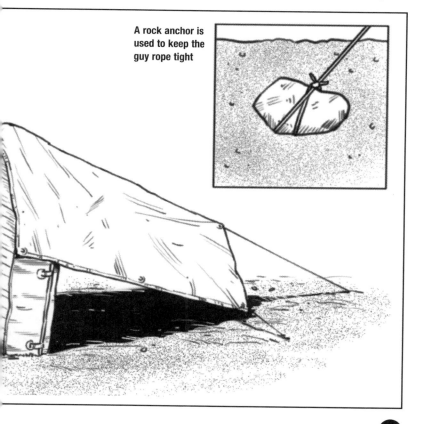

A rock anchor is used to keep the guy rope tight

Adaptable A-frame

An A-frame shelter can be covered with all manner of materials, from vegetation to snow. Make sure that the entrance to the shelter faces away from the prevailing winds, and don't build the shelter too high – the larger it is, the more space there is to heat inside.

Framework

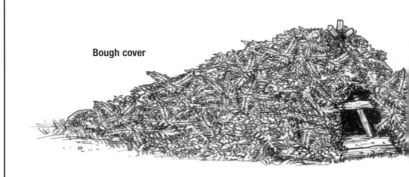

Bough cover

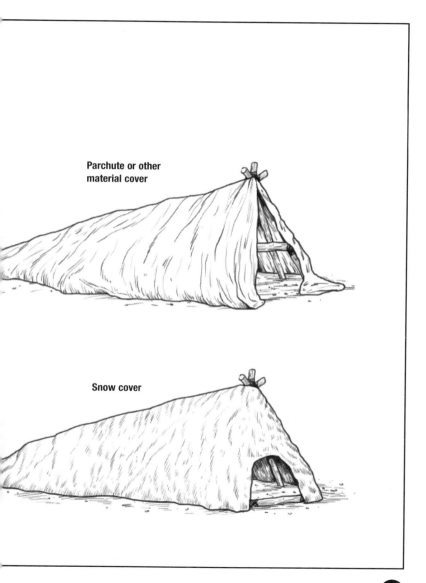

**Parchute or other
material cover**

Snow cover

Desert Shelters

Desert shelters should be constructed with a double-layer roof. This configuration traps a section of still air between the sheets, which helps prevent the transfer of the sun's heat to the interior of the shelter.

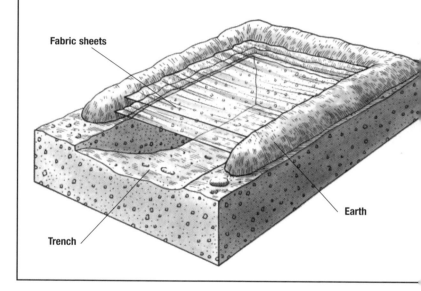

Fabric sheets

Earth

Trench

risk death or injury from a build-up of poisonous gases.

The snow cave is not the only arctic shelter option. If deep snow has built up around the base of a fir tree, you can dig down around the base of the trunk to create a chamber, while the fir branches above provide a thick, insulating

roof. You can also make a snow trench shelter by digging a trench down into the snow, insulating it with fir branches, then cutting blocks of hard snow to create walls and a roof around the trench. The limits of what you can construct often depend on the exigencies of your survival situation and your

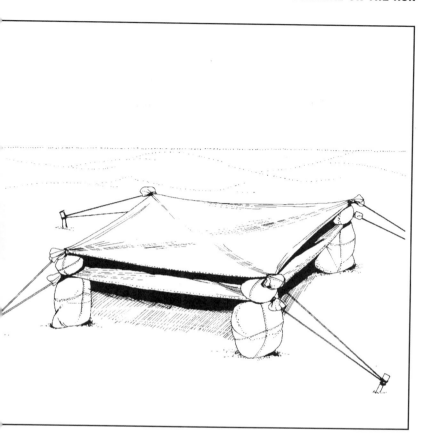

evasion goals. Of all the shelters described above, the snow cave and the tree shelter are probably the best for keeping you hidden, as they can blend easily into the landscape.

Survival on the run is one of the most demanding physical and mental challenges a human being can face. Not only does he have to cope with the threats of climate, wildlife, terrain, dehydration and starvation, he must also have enough mental stamina to maintain effective evasion techniques at all times. At some point, things are likely to go wrong, and we will now look at how the soldier can cope when the worst happens.

Tropical Shelters

The most important point about constructing tropical shelters is to build a platform off the ground. Jungle floors teem with aggressive insect and animal life, and the platform will keep you safe above it while you sleep. Bamboo is one of the most useful materials for shelter construction, although a sharp machete is needed to cut it.

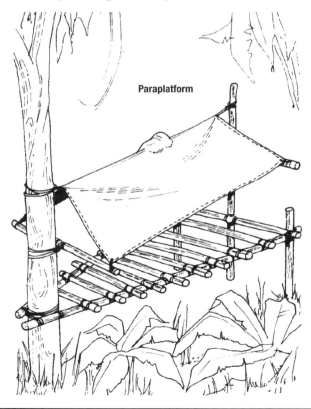

Paraplatform

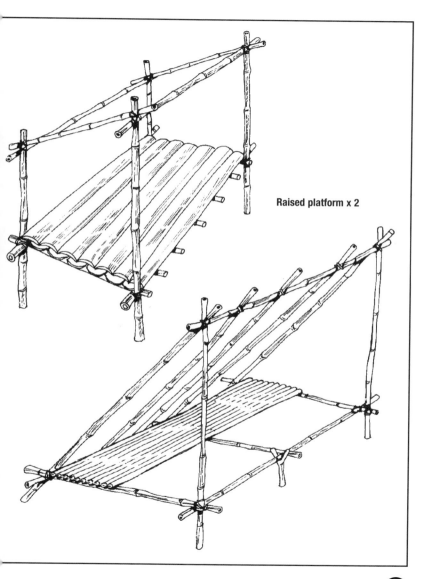

Raised platform x 2

Seashore Shelter

The combination of sand and wood used in this construction will make the final shelter extremely durable. With any seashore shelter, make sure that you construct it safely above the high-tide mark to avoid an unexpected flooding.

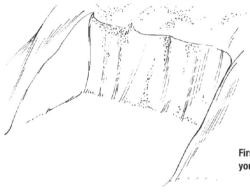

First clear the site for your seashore shelter

Build a framework using strong pieces of driftwood and other timber

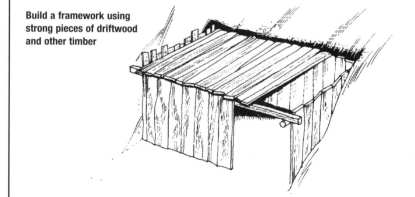

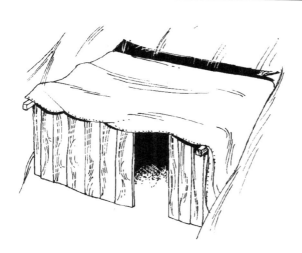

**Cover the roof with a piece of
sandproof material**

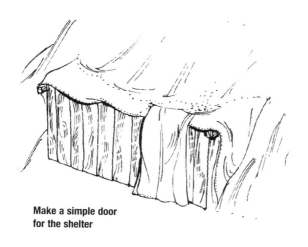

**Make a simple door
for the shelter**

Snow Cave

The two most important features of a snow cave are the ventilation holes, bored through the wall to the outside, and the sleeping platform. The latter is carved at a higher level than the rest of the shelter, meaning that warm air rises up to you while you sleep, while cold air sinks down to the sump near the door.

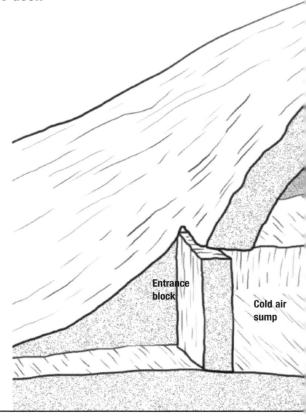

Entrance block

Cold air sump

Air vent

Sleeping
platform

Escape and evasion is an unpredictable business. As we have seen in previous chapters, actual escape from detention is just the beginning of a dangerous journey, with threats ranging from disease and injury through to a vengeful and pursuing enemy. On this basis, you have to be prepared to fight for your freedom.

Compromised

We deal first with one of the most obvious emergencies faced by a soldier attempting to evade the enemy – he is discovered by his pursuers, or by other individuals. Being 'compromised' will, in many cases, involve recapture and a return to captivity. If this is the case, obey all the early-capture procedures outlined previously in this book. Your pursuers are likely to have a renewed sense of aggression towards you, because of the inconvenience and defiance of your escape attempt, and so you will need to be compliant, hopefully to avoid excessive rough treatment or even abrupt execution.

. . . .

The dangers that face a soldier on the run include injuries, illnesses, being spotted by the enemy search and exposure to hostile elements. The evader has to be ready for anything.

5

Until an escaped prisoner reaches either safety or is rescued, his future remains uncertain. He needs a level head to cope should disaster strike.

Emergencies

Escape

Yet being compromised doesn't always involve surrender. There are two other options – escape or fight. Both possibilities depend on the nature of the threat facing you. Escape is the best option against an enemy who spots you from afar, the distance giving you some time to make further evasive manoeuvres and hopefully disappear into the wilderness. Such is also a wise move if you are compromised by civilians or by single isolated individuals. For a start, they might not even recognize you for what you are, particularly if they see you from a long way away. Therefore, if you are spotted in the open don't immediately start running or behaving nervously, but simply move casually to a place where you can disappear from view. Indeed, you can use this technique if you have no option but to cross exposed ground in view of others. Carrying a non-suspicious item, such as a spade or shopping bag, could make you appear as nothing more than a civilian on his way somewhere. This approach obviously depends on your not wearing full military uniform, another good reason to pick up any civilian items of clothing you can while conducting your evasion.

Regardless of how well you feel your impersonation has played out, once you are out of sight again treat any enemy or civilian visual contact as full compromise, no matter how seemingly innocuous the people involved. During the infamous Bravo Two Zero operation in January 1991, for example, an SAS patrol hunting SCUD missile launchers in Iraq was compromised simply by a few observant members of a Bedouin family. The Bedouin reported the sighting to the Iraqi military, who then appeared in force, and a major firefight was the outcome.

Hiding

Following compromise, therefore, a key decision you have to make is whether to run or hide. This decision has to be based on factors such as predicted time of enemy response, the strength of nearby enemy forces and whether the local area provides good cover and concealment. Sometimes simply staying put and hiding can be viable. An example of this in action is provided by Chandos Blair, a British soldier serving with the Seaforth Highlanders during World War II. Captured by the Germans during the early years of the conflict, he was imprisoned in Biberach POW camp about 121km (75 miles) from the Swiss border. In 1941, determined to escape, he systematically put together an extensive escape kit, including a homemade compass, pocket knife, a basic map of the area, a watch, four boxes of matches, three handkerchiefs, a

Blending In

Sometimes an evasion plan will actually take you right into a foreign civilian society. Observe every aspect of your surroundings – clothing, mannerisms, employment, etc – and model your behaviour so that you blend in.

EMERGENCIES

SAS Ambush

SAS soldier Chris Ryan was a member of the ill-fated Bravo Two Zero team in Iraq in 1991. During his long escape and evasion journey to the Syrian border, he fought and defeated two enemy soldiers with just a knife and his bare hands: 'My survival instinct took over – instinct sharpened by years of training. Whoever these guys were, it was going to be them or me. To fire a shot in that position would have been fatal, so I quietly laid my 203 [grenade launcher] down and got my knife open in my right hand. As the first man came level with me I grabbed him, stuck him in the neck and ripped his throat out. He went down without a sound. When the second man saw me, his eyes widened in terror and he began to run. But somehow, with a surge of adrenaline, I flew after him, jumped on him and brought him down with my legs locked around his hips. I got one arm round his neck in a judo hold and stretched his chin up. There was a muffled crack, and he died instantaneously.'
– Chris Ryan, *The One That Got Away* (Arrow Books, 2008)

shaving and washing kit, a half loaf of bread, some chocolate, cheese and dates, and a tin of Horlicks tablets. He hid his escape kit, and himself, in a pile of unused bed frames and mattresses, which were then carried outside the camp by an Allied work party and stored in a garage beyond the wire. Once night fell, Blair made his escape, heading towards the Swiss frontier and moving only at night through difficult forest terrain. After several days, however, Blair was spotted by a local boy while moving through woodland. The boy ran off, and Blair knew that it would be only a matter of time before others arrived at the scene. Thinking quickly, he simply climbed a tall tree and concealed himself in the thick branches. Sure enough, a search party arrived and scoured the woods, but they did not spot the escaped POW hiding just above them, assuming that the fugitive was bound to run. Once they had gone, Blair came down from the tree, resumed his journey, and eight days later crossed the Swiss border to freedom.

Fight

Of course, when compromised it is not always possible to escape, and in these situations the only solution might be to fight. Try this only if you have a decent chance of winning the engagement, or if the consequences of being recaptured are too

Choke Hold

**One of the most efficient ways to neutralize a human
threat silently is a choke hold. Here a forearm is used to
apply pressure to the enemy's throat, while the other arm
provides leverage against the back of his head.**

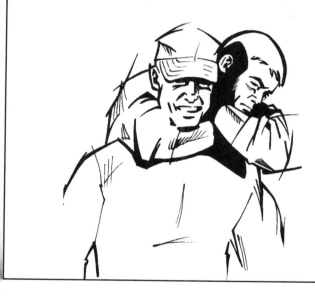

appalling as an alternative. Much
depends on your weaponry. With
just your bare hands, or basic
weapons such as a rock, club or
knife, you have limited combat
options. In such circumstances, try
to ambush individual soldiers at
points where they are separated from
larger groups. Attempt to take them
down with violence that is as silent
as possible – a blow on the head
with a large rock to send them
instantly unconscious, a knife attack
to the throat to sever their windpipe,
or a choking attack.

If you have acquired a firearm or
other weapon, the odds of your
survival in an engagement are
dramatically improved. Make sure
you rule out other attack methods

Tackling a Rifleman from the Rear

Disposing of an armed guard needs to be done quickly and ruthlessly. Here the evader grabs the guard from behind, pulls him down to the ground and delivers a powerful chopping blow to the throat, targeting the windpipe.

A

B

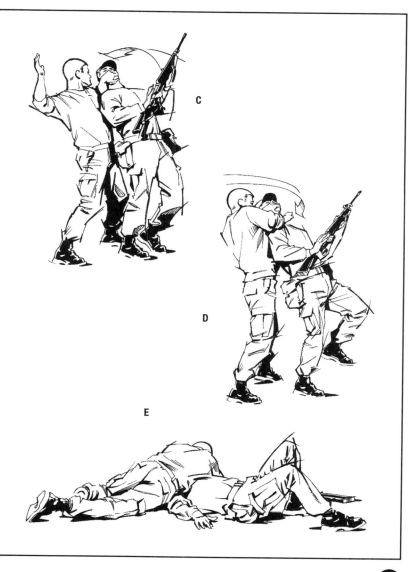

C

D

E

Tip: How to Load and Fire an AK-47 Assault Rifle

The AK-47, and its variants, are the most extensively distributed weapons in history. If the AK isn't your standard firearm, you should take time to learn exactly how one works, in case you acquire one during escape and evasion. The following are official US Army instructions for using the AK:

Loading the magazine:
Place a round between the feed lips (A). Press it down until it locks inside the magazine. Repeat until magazine is full.

Inserting the magazine into the receiver:
Tip the magazine forward so the lug on the front of the magazine engages with its recess in the magazine well; then pull the magazine to the rear until it snaps into place (B).

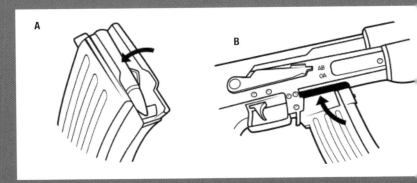

Firing the AK-47:
Place the selector (C) on the desired position (automatic middle
position, semi-automatic lower position). Aim using a normal sight
picture and pull the trigger. The AK-47 with the metal stock can also
be fired with the stock folded. This is done by pressing the stock latch
located on the left rear of the receiver, swinging the stock down
beneath the weapon (D). This position is used mainly by airborne and
armor units.

Unloading:
Remove the magazine by pressing the magazine catch toward the
magazine; then swing the magazine forward and out of the receiver.
Pull the operating handle fully to the rear, inspect the chamber and
receiver. If no cartridge is present, release the operating handle and
pull the trigger.

– *Department of the Army/203d Military Intelligence Battalion,
Operator's Manual for AK-47 Assault Rifle*

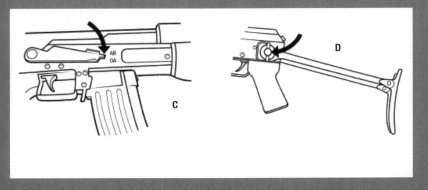

first. A ripping burst of automatic fire, or a grenade explosion, will be heard for many miles around, and will likely attract larger forces to the area. If you have no choice, then try to attack at an opportune moment, such as when enemy troops have downed their weapons during a break, or when they are funnelled into a narrow 'kill zone' in the terrain. Remember that the enemy will typically head towards the point at which you were last spotted, so you have the chance of preparing an ambush.

There are several other circumstances in which you might have to use violence to keep your evasion plan on course. You might, for example, have to kill a sentry to cross through a checkpoint area. Nevertheless, try to avoid such actions if at all possible. Not only will a dead body provide an emphatic piece of 'sign' to your pursuers, it is also likely to galvanize their efforts further, with an intention of exacting revenge.

Caught in the Middle

Another significant danger to the escaped prisoner is that presented by his own side. If the evader is moving through an active combat zone, he is exposed to becoming 'collateral damage' in the fighting between the two sides. In modern warfare, much killing is done remotely, by artillery, missile systems and air power (including unmanned

Taking Cover

As an evader gets closer to his own lines, he may well be threatened by his 'friendly' artillery and air strikes. As he will have learnt in basic training, the important point to survival in these situations is to get low behind substantial cover. Remember that shrapnel retains lethality hundreds of metres from the explosion.

US Army Tip: Reacting to Aerial Flares

The enemy might deploy aerial flares in an attempt to spot you at night. The following is official US Army advice about what to do if you are caught in the glare:

- If you hear the firing of an aerial flare while you are moving, hit the ground (behind cover if possible) while the flare is rising and before it bursts and illuminates.
- If moving where it is easy to blend with the background (such as in a forest) and you are caught in the light of an aerial flare, freeze in place until the flare burns out.
- If you are caught in the light of an aerial flare while moving in an open area, immediately crouch low or lie down.
- If you are crossing an obstacle, such as a barbed-wire fence or a wall, and get caught in the light of an aerial flare, crouch low and stay down until the flare burns out.
- The sudden light of a bursting flare may temporarily blind both you and the enemy. When the enemy uses a flare to spot you, he spoils his own night vision. To protect your night vision, close one eye while the flare is burning. When the flare burns out, the eye that was closed will still have its night vision.

aerial vehicles – UAVs). In this environment, heavily reliant upon computer datafeed from various surveillance systems, it is not always easy to separate friend from foe, particularly if someone is viewing you through a grainy computer monitor or infra-red device. If you have altered your appearance to appear like an enemy soldier, and are carrying foreign weapons, then the chances of you being targeted as a 'hostile' are that much greater. For this reason, you are better maintaining a 'neutral' appearance when you are around the frontlines; this way you might avoid being interpreted as a threat by your own side.

Obviously, try to avoid areas where fighting is intense. Also be careful about exposing yourself to friendly air assets if they are attacking local enemy forces. The crew of an Apache helicopter hitting a nearby convoy, for example, will be making rapid target acquisition and firing decisions, and the sudden appearance of someone waving his hands in the air might not lead them to conclude that you are an escaped POW. Instead of their flying in to rescue you, they might simply give you a burst from their Chain Gun. Try instead to reach a safe location, away from the immediate battlefront, before identifying yourself to air assets. Not only will the safer environment for the aircraft give them an opportunity to study you more carefully, they might even be able to mount an immediate rescue operation.

As a trained soldier, you might also need to rely on your basic training if you come under shellfire, gunfire and aerial bombardment, regardless of the provenance of the fire. The rules of finding cover apply in these situations, which will have been ingrained through training and possibly operational experience. Should the fire be from your own side, use your knowledge of 'friendly' weapons to provide further guidance to your actions. For example, if you see nearby enemy positions being hit by aerial munitions, carefully note the time of the strike (if you have a watch), the type of target being hit and, if you

can see it, the aircraft making the strike. If you can then establish comms with your own side, you can provide the details of the air strike, and intelligence officers will then be able to cross-reference your report with post-strike data to confirm your location. If the aircraft were dropping Joint Direct Attack Munition (JDAM) GPS-guided munitions, or similar guided weapons, then the location fix on your position can be very accurate indeed.

Medical Emergencies

Medical emergencies are the most critical issues that can face anyone while conducting escape and evasion, and therefore make up the bulk of this chapter. The unfortunate fact is that a person who has just escaped from a POW camp, or has been shot down in an aircraft, is unlikely to be in peak physical condition. Often in a weakened state, the individual is susceptible to further injury or illness from environmental effects, or from a serious drop in food or fluid intake. More dramatically, the evader is also exposed to the threats presented by the enemy himself – bullets, bombs, shells – with the added danger that any injury sustained won't be treated immediately by a friendly medic.

A comprehensive guide to military first aid is impossible here; a good first aid course is part of basic training for many soldiers, and if it

Gunshot Wound

Gunshot wounds can be extremely complicated injuries to treat. Not only can the bullet take an irregular route through the body, bouncing off bones and fragmenting, it can also create an exit wound much larger than the entrance wound. Treat all external injuries and monitor the casualty for signs of shock.

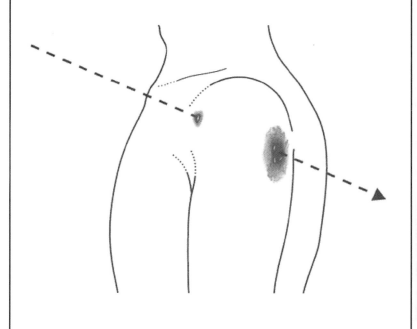

Pressure Points

Pressure points are locations on the body – shown by the
nodules here – that can be pressed with the fingers to
control major arterial bleeding. Pressure-point treatment
is short-term only; anything more than a few minutes
risks damaging tissue by cutting off blood supply entirely.

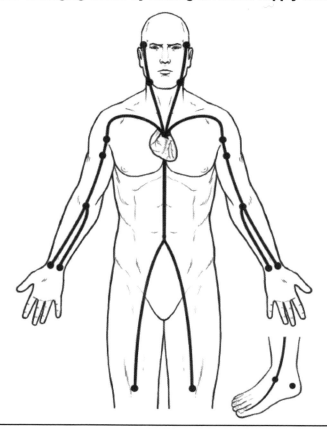

isn't, the soldier should seek it out. Here we will instead look at some of the essential treatments for a few common injury types, principally in the context of self-treatment. Although escape and evasion can and has taken place in small groups or in pairs, it is often conducted by a single individual working on his own. In this situation, an evader has to monitor his or her own health, and implement self-treatment in the case of illness or injury. Such is far from easy, and it requires a very honest approach to self-analysis. No matter how tough you are, you can't argue with either physics or biology. For example, if you are bleeding heavily, and your blood volume drops below safe levels, you will slip into shock, unconsciousness and possibly death. Similarly, if you find yourself inadequately dressed in a freezing environment, you have to take drastic action, or you will succumb to hypothermia. Don't overestimate your powers of endurance, and take immediate action to stop a bad situation getting worse. This principle might even involve giving yourself up to the enemy, in the hope that you will receive full medical treatment.

Bleeding injuries

The threat from serious bleeding injuries comes in the form of circulatory (not psychological) shock. Shock has several different possible

Chest Dressing

Chest wounds can be dangerous because the ingress of air into the chest cavity can cause the lungs to collapse. This chest bandage – taped on three sides only – acts like a simple one-way valve, keeping air out but letting it escape from the chest as the casualty breathes.

causes, but the effect is a significant and life-threatening, drop in the oxygenation of body tissue. Bleeding injuries can result in shock by loss of blood, which can lead to a dangerous drop in blood pressure. A loss of about 15 per cent of blood

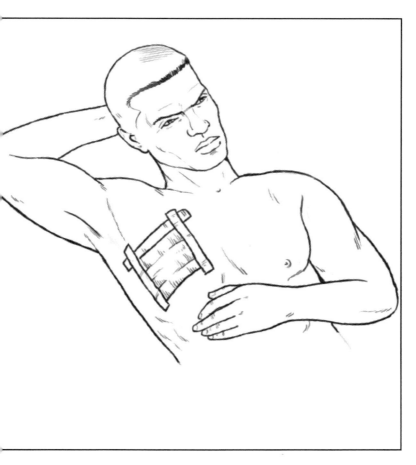

volume results in symptoms such as weakness, nausea, disorientation, dizziness, fainting, clammy skin and rapid heartbeat. If the blood loss is stopped there, and the casualty is able to rest afterwards, a full recovery should be made as long as there are no complicating issues. If the blood loss reaches beyond 30 per cent, the situation is far more serious, as the body's compensatory mechanisms begin to fail and the casualty descends towards unconsciousness, organ damage and (at around 50 per cent volume loss) death.

As soon as you sustain a bleeding injury, follow the simple rule of applying firm, direct pressure to the wound site with a clean pad of material (or one as clean as possible). If no such pad is available, then use your hand. Keep the pressure up until the bleeding stops, a process that may take many minutes if the injury is severe enough. Should the blood soak through the pad, don't remove the pad but place another one on top and maintain the pressure. Also, if there is a foreign object stuck in the wound, do not attempt to remove it, but instead apply pressure around the object until the bleeding stops. For bleeding injuries on a limb, try to elevate the limb above the level of your heart, to reduce blood pressure at the wound site and make it easier to stop the bleeding.

Once you have controlled the blood loss, you should clean the wound as much as possible, carefully picking out dirt and debris, and then bandage it with a clean dressing. (Don't pull out anything that will restart the bleeding.) When applying a bandage, ensure that you don't tie it too tight so that you

Sutures

Some survival medical kits will contain various types of sutures for stitching wounds. Here we see, on the left, the traditional type of knotted stitch, while on the right we have adhesive sutures. Any stitched wound needs to be monitored closely for infection developing.

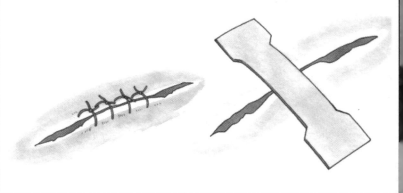

US Army Survival Tip: Health and Hygiene

a. Stay clean (daily regimen).
  (1) Minimize infection by washing. (Use white ashes, sand, or loamy soil as soap substitutes.)
  (2) Comb and clean debris from hair.
  (3) Cleanse mouth and brush teeth.
    (a) Use hardwood twig as toothbrush (fray it by chewing on one end then use as brush).
    (b) Use single strand of an inner core string from parachute cord for dental floss.
    (c) Use clean finger to stimulate gum tissues by rubbing.
    (d) Gargle with salt water to help prevent sore throat and aid in cleaning teeth and gums.
  (4) Clean and protect feet.
    (a) Change and wash socks
    (b) Wash, dry, and massage.
    (c) Check frequently for blisters and red areas.
    (d) Use adhesive tape/mole skin to prevent damage.
b. Exercise daily.
c. Prevent and control parasites.
  (1) Check body for lice, fleas, ticks, etc.
    (a) Check body regularly.
    (b) Pick off insects and eggs (DO NOT crush).
  (2) Wash clothing and use repellents.
  (3) Use smoke to fumigate clothing and equipment.

– Survival, Escape, and Evasion (1999)

cut off circulation. To test that circulation is still working in an injured limb, pinch a toenail or fingernail on that limb until it goes white; when you release the pressure, the nail should go pink again as the blood flow returns. If the nail stays white, the bandage needs to be relaxed.

Heat Exhaustion/Stroke

Someone with heat exhaustion (left) can exhibit sweaty, flushed skin and dilated pupils. If his condition advances to heat stroke (right), the sweating might stop, the skin go pale and the pupils constrict.

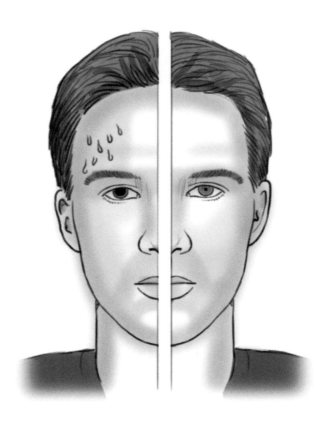

Following a tissue injury, a key priority is to prevent infection establishing itself. Indications of infection include: a throbbing pain at the wound site; leakage of blood and pus; a bad smell emanating from the wound; and general feelings of illness. If left unattended, the infection can turn into gangrene or blood poisoning, with potentially fatal consequences.

Prevent infection by keeping the wound as clean as possible. Wash around the wound carefully with soap and water (do not scrub the wound itself, or allow soap to enter it), and irrigate the injury with plenty of fresh water. Replace soiled dressings with clean ones. Cut away pieces of skin or fat that have evidently died – they will have turned black or blue. If there are signs of infection, apply hot compresses to the wound site to draw out the malady. Wrap boiled and mashed substances such as potatoes, rice or tree bark in a cloth and apply to the wound; try to make the poultice as hot as you can stand. Wash away pus with warm salt water. If you can't control the infection, and you start to feel seriously ill, then your only option might be to turn yourself in.

Heat and cold
A bleeding injury, such as caused by a knife or gunshot, is an instantly recognizable threat. (Having said this, do make sure you inspect your own body thoroughly after a violent encounter, in case you have picked up any injuries you weren't aware of at the time.) More insidious but just as serious, however, are the injuries that can accrue from the effects of extreme cold and extreme heat.

Heat exhaustion/heat stroke
In terms of hot-climate injuries, the major threats are heat exhaustion and heat stroke. Heat exhaustion is generated by dehydration, the casualty's fluid intake being exceeded by his fluid loss, particularly through sweating. The symptoms include:

- Excessive sweating.
- Pale, moist, cool skin.
- Feelings of weakness.
- Tingling hands and/or feet.
- Dizziness.
- Confusion.
- The urge to defecate.
- Loss of appetite.
- Headache.
- Cramping.
- Nausea.
- Chills.
- Rapid breathing.

Heat stroke shares many of the same symptoms as heat exhaustion, but on a more severe scale. It is caused when the core internal body temperature of around 37.0°C (98.6°F) rises above safe parameters, and is precipitated by a failure in the body's cooling

Cooling the Casualty

One method of cooling a
heat stroke victim is to wrap
him in a sheet and keep the
sheet soaked with cool (not
ice cold) water, refreshing
the water regularly as the
casualty's body warms it up.

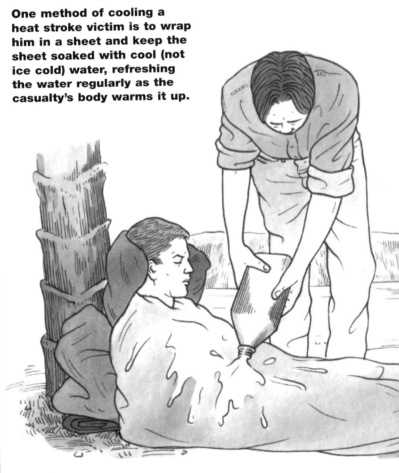

mechanisms. It can be accompanied by a rapid and weak pulse, and might lead to sudden collapse and unconsciousness, and death.

Heat-related illnesses are often generally easier to recognize in others than in oneself, but the important point is to act quickly as soon as even the mildest symptoms described start to emerge – prevention is always better than cure. Get out of the sun immediately and into shade, then lie down and loosen your clothing. Take many frequent sips of water to rehydrate your system.

For heat stroke, if water is available, such as from a nearby stream, soak your clothing or skin regularly; as the water evaporates from the surface of your skin, it will take body heat away with it. You must rest, as your body is in a weakened state and further exertions could lead to a heart attack or other serious consequence.

Hypothermia and frostbite

Like heat injuries, cold injuries can creep up gradually on the casualty, and create a mental confusion that masks the reality of what is happening. Freezing air temperatures are dangerous enough in their own right, but their potential lethality is magnified by the effects of windchill and wet weather, both of which accelerate a person's heat loss.

The US armed services' *Survival,*

Taking Shelter

Whether in cold or hot climates, shelter is a priority for anyone trying to survive extreme weather. Shelters needn't be sophisticated; here the evader simply hollows out a cave in the soil of a bank, but it is sufficient to get him out of wind and rain.

Evasion, and Recovery manual lists some of the other common factors that may result in a person being afflicted by cold injuries. They are:

- *In contact with the ground (such as marching, performing guard duty, or engaging in other outside activities).*
- *Immobile for long periods (such as while riding in an unheated or open vehicle).*
- *Standing in water, such as in a foxhole.*
- *Out in the cold for days without being warmed.*
- *Deprived of an adequate diet and rest.*
- *Not able to take care of his personal hygiene.*

We can see from this list how someone conducting escape and evasion might be particularly vulnerable to cold injuries. A person escaping through a frozen wilderness might find himself lying still in a hole-up, unable to light a fire and in

contact with the frozen ground, while already weak and undernourished.

The priorities in terms of prevention are to stay as warm and dry as possible, changing wet clothing for dry clothing as regularly as possible. Try to find a location in which you can light a fire for warmth, and aim to consume at least one hot meal or drink a day. When the weather is particularly aggressive, such as heavy snowfall or driving cold rain, seek or make shelter if you have inadequate clothing. Take plenty of rest.

Hypothermia is the real killer in the cold. It is the reverse of heat stroke, and occurs when the core body temperature drops to unsafe levels. Early symptoms include intense shivering, and simple tasks become complicated to perform as the body draws blood away from the brain to protect core processes. The shivering can increase, and then stop, as the symptoms worsen, and speech and thinking degrade further. Collapse, coma and death can follow if you haven't acted by this stage.

US Army Tip: Trench Foot – How to Avoid it

'Trench foot', also known as 'immersion foot', is a serious condition that results from feet suffering prolonged exposure to damp, cold and dirty conditions. It produces skin rotting, blisters, sores, fungal infections and even gangrene, and can lead to amputation. The official US military advice for prevention is as follows, and should be put into action if the skin appears waxy and wrinkled:

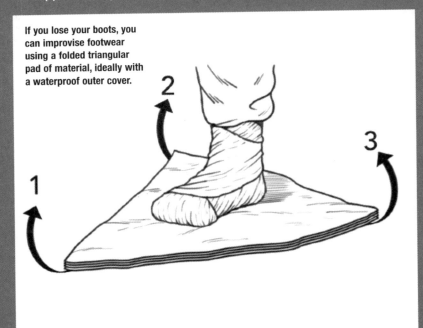

If you lose your boots, you can improvise footwear using a folded triangular pad of material, ideally with a waterproof outer cover.

(a) Avoid walking on affected feet.
(b) Pat dry; DO NOT rub. Skin tissue will be sensitive.
(c) Dry socks and shoes. Keep feet protected.
(d) Loosen boots, cuffs, etc., to improve circulation.
(e) Keep area dry, warm, and open to air.
(f) DO NOT apply creams or ointments.

– *Survival, Evasion, and Recovery* (1999)

Gaiters are a good way of keeping the feet dry, although make sure that they are replaced if they become soaked.

During the SAS Bravo Two Zero operation in 1991, hypothermia started to affect all the members of the team deployed when unseasonal snowstorms swept through the Iraqi desert. Chris Ryan noted that 'I'd had plenty of lectures on hypothermia, and now I recognized some of the symptoms in myself: disorientation, dizziness, sudden mood swings, outbursts of anger, confusion, drowsiness.' He also noted how navigation was becoming a problem because the mental challenge of using a map and compass became too much for a freezing mind. In total, two of eight patrol members were killed by hypothermia.

As soon as you experience any of the above symptoms, get into shelter fast, build a fire and get warm. Remove wet clothing in particular, and use a sleeping bag if you have one. If you do have a companion, cuddle up close together to share body heat. If you haven't, adopt a foetal position, wrapping your arms around your legs and breathing out down onto your chest – your warm outbreaths will become trapped between your chest and bent legs, helping your torso warm up. Try to cover yourself with a coat, blanket or similar protection, and make sure that you are insulated from the ground by other items of clothing or a thick layer of vegetation. If you can warm up some stones in a fire, wrap them in cloth (so you don't burn yourself) and place them on your groin, armpits and around your neck, to help raise your blood temperature. Don't do any strenuous exercise.

Another threat from the cold is that of frostbite. This condition literally occurs when the water content of body tissue freezes solid, and it mainly attacks the vulnerable extremities – toes, fingers and ears. A prelude to frostbite is often frostnip, a loss of circulation in the outer layers of skin resulting in skin that is cold and stiff to touch, and either grey or white in white-skinned people, or pink or red in dark-skinned people. You must re-warm the affected area as soon as possible, putting it in dry clothing and holding it near a heat source. The skin should return to normal in a matter of minutes.

If your cold injury develops into full-blown frostbite, the situation is far more serious. The skin will be ice cold (often ice crystals are literally visible on the surface of the skin), blue or white in colour, heavy, immobile and completely numb. Professional medical treatment is really your only serious option, but in extreme circumstances you might have to try to defrost the injury yourself. This should not be done lightly, as frostbitten skin is extremely susceptible to further injury, and you also run the risk of blood poisoning or other infections. If you have no choice, however, the best method of defrosting the skin is to immerse it in warm water (replenished as it gets cold), allowing the skin to thaw. The procedure is painful in the extreme, and once the digit is defrosted avoid putting it under any pressure and never allow it to refreeze, which will probably destroy the tissue entirely.

Broken bones

On 26 August 1967, US Air Force major George 'Bud' Day was shot down in his F-100F Super Sabre during a raid over North Vietnam.

During the crash, Day's right arm was broken in three places, plus he had a twisted knee and a damaged eye. He was captured by local Vietnamese militia, and over the next few days was beaten and tortured. Despite his unpromising situation, he was already looking for opportunities to escape, the South Vietnamese border being within viable walking distance.

On 2 September, he made a break for it. He had convinced the guards that he was injured beyond possibility

Splinting

A splint is basically a system to immobilize an injured limb, to prevent further damage occurring. The man on the left has an injured arm splinted with a piece of wood, while the man on the right, with a broken leg, is splinted with two poles and extra bindings around his torso.

Tourniquets

A tourniquet is only to be used as a last resort, typically in the case of major traumatic amputation, when the casualty is in danger of bleeding to death in minutes. The method here utilizes a knotted cloth and a stick

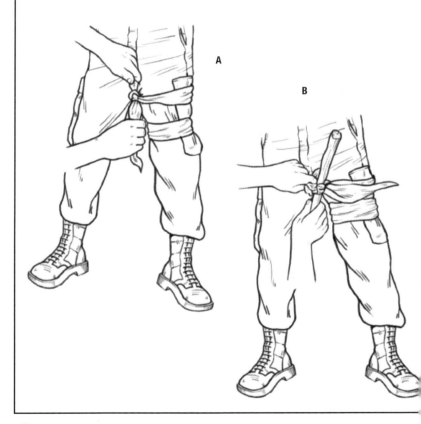

A

B

to shut off the blood supply to the injured limb. It is for this very reason that tourniquets must be used only in extremis, as they can cause tissue death in a healthy limb.

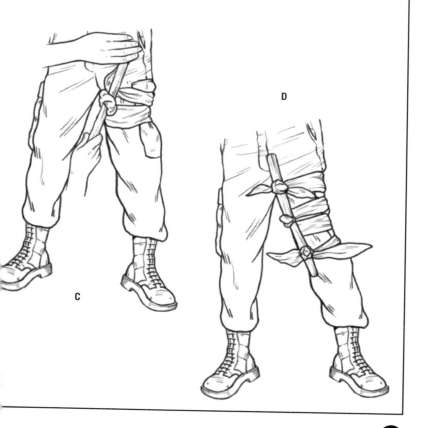

C

D

Arm Bandage

This simple triangular arm bandage can be used to support a broken arm or, by folding more of the material around the arm joint, a damaged elbow. An additional bandage could be wrapped around the torso, over the top of the arm bandage, to prevent the arm swinging when the casualty is walking.

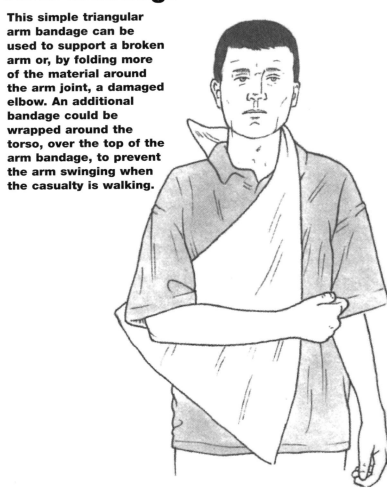

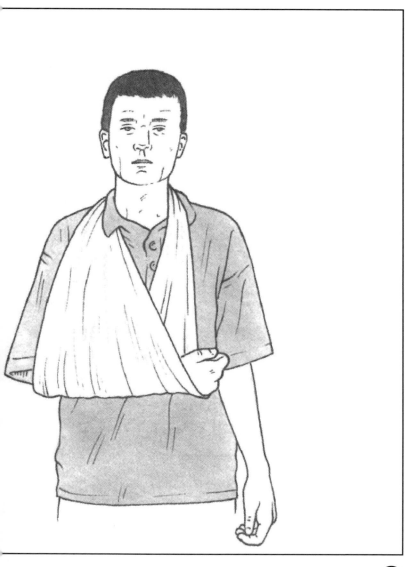

of escape, so they neglected to keep an eye on him. At the right moment he untied his bonds, stole a canteen of water, and set off into the jungle. There he survived for two weeks, living off berries, citrus fruit and frogs, and off water found in palm trees. At one point, he floated across the Ben Hai river in an improvised raft made from bamboo logs and branches – an NVA sentry saw the raft, but likely concluded that it was just driftwood.

Day made it to within a few miles of freedom, but when trying to signal a US O-1 aircraft near the South Vietnamese border, he was spotted by a VC patrol, which opened fire and injured him in the left thigh and left hand. He was thereafter taken into captivity, where he would remain until March 1973.

Day's escape effort is rendered remarkable by the fact that he made it with a virtually untreated broken arm. Such is proof that willpower can be a powerful force over adversity, even in the face of excruciating pain. Yet there is no denying that broken bones are a serious survival emergency, removing the use of a limb and raising the risk of post-fracture infection. Furthermore, without professional medical help, there is little chance of the injury healing properly.

There are two main types of bone fracture in adult humans: open and closed. With an 'open' fracture, the end of a broken bone breaks through the skin, creating a bleeding wound, while a closed fracture remains inside the flesh.

Rules for Avoiding Illness

a. Purify all water obtained from natural sources by using iodine tablets, bleach, or boiling for 5 minutes.
b. Locate latrines 200 feet [60m] from water and away from shelter.
c. Wash hands before preparing food or water.
d. Clean all eating utensils after each meal.
e. Prevent insect bites by using repellent, netting, and clothing.
f. Dry wet clothing as soon as possible.
g. Eat a varied diet.
h. Try to get 7–8 hours sleep per day.

– *Survival, Evasion, and Recovery* (1999)

Types of Fracture

There are numerous different types of fracture, as the illustration here demonstrates. In terms of survival first aid, the most important distinction is between the closed and open fracture, and the priority is always to stabilize the injury until you can reach professional medical help, when the break can be set properly.

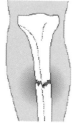

Simple fracture

Greenstick fracture

Comminuted fracture

Closed fracture

Open fracture

Roller Bandage

Roller bandages are useful dressings, and can be applied either on their own for bleeding injuries or combined with a splint (right) to immobilize a broken limb. The important point about roller bandages is that they are not too tight, or

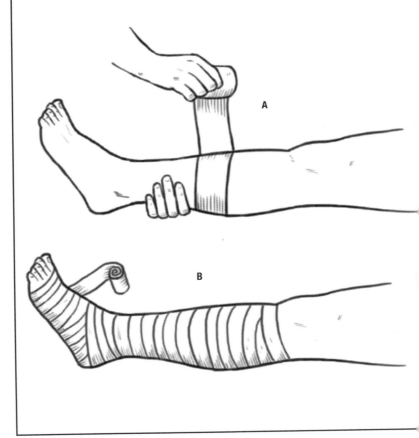

A

B

they risk cutting off the circulation to a limb. Once
the bandage is applied, pinch the fingernails or
toenails on the affected limb, and ensure that they
go pink again when released, indicating blood flow.

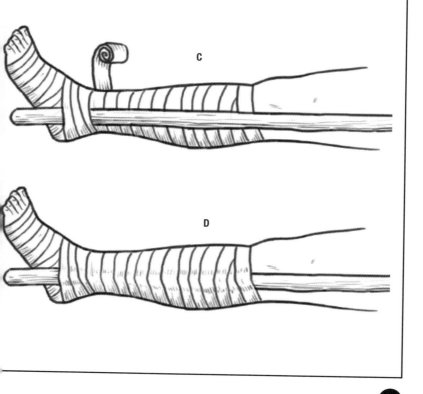

C

D

Aligning a Broken Leg

Aligning a fractured limb should be done only if professional medical help isn't available, and if the fracture is affecting nerve function or circulation. Pull firmly but smoothly on the injured limb until it is in its natural alignment, then release the pressure gently.

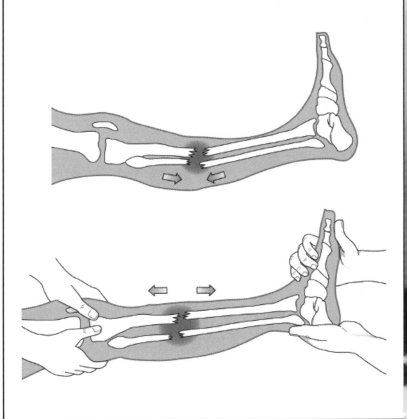

Whatever the case, you will be in little doubt as to when a fracture has occurred:

- There is often an audible sound of a bone breaking, and you will feel the bone snap.
- There is a severe pain, followed by an acute tenderness around the injury site.
- A limb or joint may be noticeably deformed, and will have a partial or complete loss of movement.
- There may be a grating sound or sensation produced by the broken ends of the bone rubbing together.
- Muscles around the injury site may go into spasm.

If you suffer an open fracture, the immediate goal of first aid is to control the bleeding in the manner described above, putting pressure around the ends of the bone rather than on top of them. With both open and closed fractures, another priority is to stabilize the injury with bandages and splints. Do this by splinting the break either side with two rigid struts (such as thick branches or poles), bandaged firmly into place. Note that this is extremely difficult to do by yourself, so it will almost certainly involve the help of a third party. In the ghastly Hanoi Hilton prison, for example, George Day had his arm splinted and bandaged by none other than fellow inmate John McCain, although the brutal Vietnamese guards often took pleasure in twisting or rebreaking the injury.

Fractures of both types can press against nerves and blood vessels, resulting – if left untreated – in nerve or circulatory damage that in extreme cases can result in the eventual loss of the limb. Such problems should be treated by medical professionals only. If you are confident that you can reach help quickly, simply stabilize the injury and keep moving towards your goal. If professional treatment is not likely for some time, however, you should try to release pressure on nerves and blood vessels by realigning the bones into their natural configuration via traction. (Do not apply traction to fractures directly on joints. These are best protected by being placed and supported in a position in the midpoint of their normal range of movement.)

Here we will describe the act of applying traction to an external casualty, but you can always give instructions to another individual if you are in fact the casualty. First, have the casualty lie down and get him to relax the muscles of the broken limb. Pull gently but firmly on the lower section of the limb, drawing it away, then angling it back towards the original line of the bone. This process can take 10–15 minutes, as you are pulling against the resistance of the muscle, and you may have to obtain extra leverage by placing the casualty against a tree or other stable feature, against which you can push while performing the traction.

For open fractures, clean the exposed bone and wound first before applying traction, and take care that you don't trap any skin as the bone is moved back under the flesh. When the traction has been performed properly, the broken limb should be in a natural alignment and nerve signals and blood flow should be restored. Then splint the injury to

prevent its moving again in transit. The process of traction can also be applied to dislocation injuries, to relocate displaced joints such as shoulder, hips and fingers into their original configuration.

Space here means that we have mainly focused on the implications of dealing with fractured limbs. There are many other bones in the body that can be fractured, including major structures such as the pelvis and skull. Such breaks require professional medical treatment, with few survival first aid options.

Treating Burns

Your main goal when treating a burn is to reduce the heat of the burn as soon as possible through dousing the wound with cool water (A). Remember to remove any rings or other items of jewellery from the affected area (B). Wrap the injury in a clean material bandage (C).

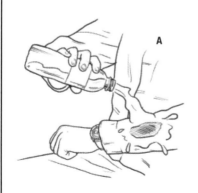
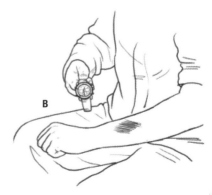

Burns

Burns are another hazard of survival, the threats ranging from scalding yourself on a camp fire through to being caught in incendiary explosions. As injuries, burns can vary enormously in severity, from minor skin redness and blistering through to complete destruction of subcutaneous tissue, bone and muscle. Whatever the cause of the burn, your overriding goal is to reduce the heat of the burn immediately – even if the cause of burn is no longer present, the heat that caused the injury will continue to cause tissue damage unless it is cooled. To do this, douse the wound with copious amounts of cool (not iced or near-freezing) water for at least 10 minutes. Don't remove any clothing that is embedded in or stuck onto the flesh, because doing so will induce bleeding and increase the severity of the injury. Remove, if you can, any rings, watches, jewellery or tight clothing from around the burn area, as the tissue will begin to swell from the injury and the constricting items will hamper circulation. Do not apply any lotions or greases, and handle the burnt area gently, as the tissue is very fragile.

Once you have cooled the burn, wrap the injury in a clean, non-fluffy material. Burnt hands or feet can be protected by being placed into a clear plastic bag, bound gently at the wrist or ankle. Note that the healing process with severe burns is also quite intensive in its consumption of body fluids, so ensure that you increase your uptake of water.

Our all-too-brief journey through some of the fundamentals of survival first aid reminds us that the ultimate objective of escape and evasion is to reach safe hands. The longer that you spend on the run in the wilderness, the greater the chances of your capture or injury. This is why, in our final chapter, we turn to the most important objective of escape and evasion – finding your way home.

C

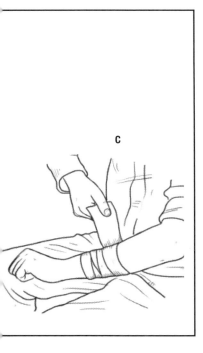

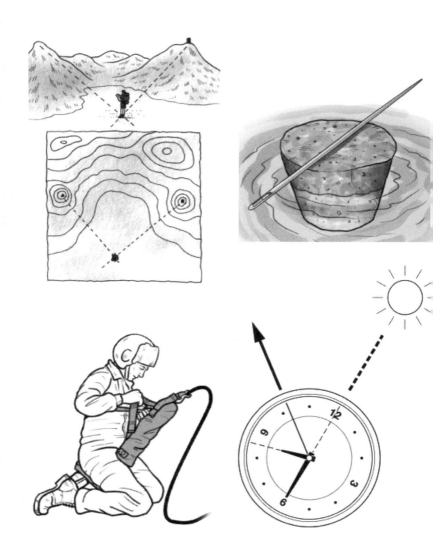

The ultimate goal of escape and evasion is to get home. For all the discussion of evasion techniques in earlier chapters, being on the run is not an objective in itself, but a phase that must be kept as short as possible. In this chapter, therefore, we look at the 'home run', or how to make the final transition to safety and freedom. As we shall see, there are distinct dangers in this phase, and the lesson to keep in mind is that you are not entirely safe until you are finally in the hands of friendly forces.

The Plan

During any escape and evasion action, it is imperative that you form a clear idea of where you are going, and how you intend to reach safety. Your evasion plan should, in essence, take you on the most direct route to safety, while at the same time allowing for the inevitable detours around hostile forces and treacherous terrain. Several options present themselves:

- You could attempt to cross through border areas into a friendly or allied country.

. . . .

Finding your way to safety through enemy territory requires skills in navigation, either by using man-made navigational aids or utilizing the information provided by nature.

6

The final goal of any soldier on the run is to make it back into the hands of his own side. The last stages of evasion, however, can be the most dangerous.

The Home Run

Evasion Corridor

An evasion corridor is a planned route through enemy territory from a start point to a final destination. Defining an evasion corridor allows soldiers to identify where they want to be on each day, and it should be distributed to rescue forces before commencing an operation.

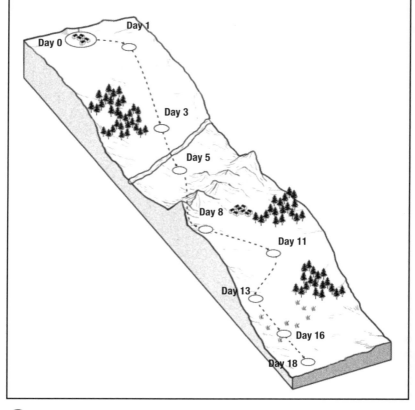

Day 0
Day 1
Day 3
Day 5
Day 8
Day 11
Day 13
Day 16
Day 18

- You could pass through an active combat zone, to reach your side's frontline.
- You could establish communications with rescue forces, and call in a rescue team.
- You could signal for help when the possibility of rescue presents itself.

All these options will be considered in detail in this chapter. Whichever you choose, however, it has to be viable within the context of present threats and your physical state. Chris Ryan, the SAS soldier mentioned in the previous chapter, made a 300km (186-mile) journey on foot through the freezing, then scorching, Iraqi desert before he crossed the Syrian border and made it to safety. The physical toll of this journey was profound. In addition to losing 16kg (35lb) in weight, Ryan noted that: 'To this day my gums haven't fully recovered; some teeth are still loose [an effect of malnutrition] ... It took six weeks for feeling to come back to my fingers and toes ... I had a blood disorder, caused by drinking dirty water from the Euphrates, as well as an abnormal amount of enzymes in my liver produced in reaction to poisoning.' Nevertheless, he went on to make virtually a full recovery, but his experience shows that only someone who begins such a journey in peak physical fitness is likely to make it.

Another important ingredient in Ryan's epic evasion was his ability to navigate, to keep going in the right direction to reach the Syrian border. Deserts in particular can be extremely difficult environments in which to find and keep a bearing – featureless expanses, heat mirages and shifting, sandy terrain making route plotting a challenge. Yet navigation in any terrain can be problematic if you don't have good navigational equipment and a decent map. Subtle shifts in your direction of travel, imperceptible as they are happening, can eventually put you dozens of miles away from where you want to be, and can actually take you deeper into danger. Hence you need to know some basic methods of improvised navigation to ensure that your rescue plan works.

Navigation

The ideal situation for any evader is to have professional navigational equipment – such as a compass, large-scale map and GPS device. This advantageous position is possible if a soldier has managed to take the equipment with him when initially separated from his unit. If he has been through a POW camp or a hostage cell, however, he is unlikely to have been able to retain any of these pieces of kit, and will therefore have to rely on more primitive methods of establishing location and direction.

Compass Bearing

Lay one edge of the compass baseplate along the line of travel that you want to follow, with the direction of travel arrow pointing in the direction you want to go. Rotate the compass housing (ignoring the needle) until the orienting lines are parallel to the grid lines. Correct for declination, and the compass is now set to show the course to your chosen destination.

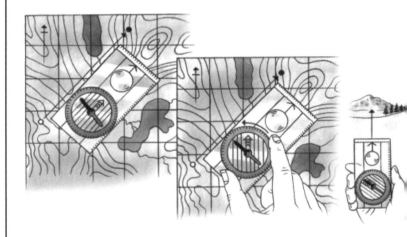

Resection

Resection is a way of fixing your position by using two or more intersecting compass bearings. Choose landmarks that lie around 90 degrees apart (A), as this minimizes the area of potential error in your position fix. A narrower angle (B), or a broader one, increases the potential error.

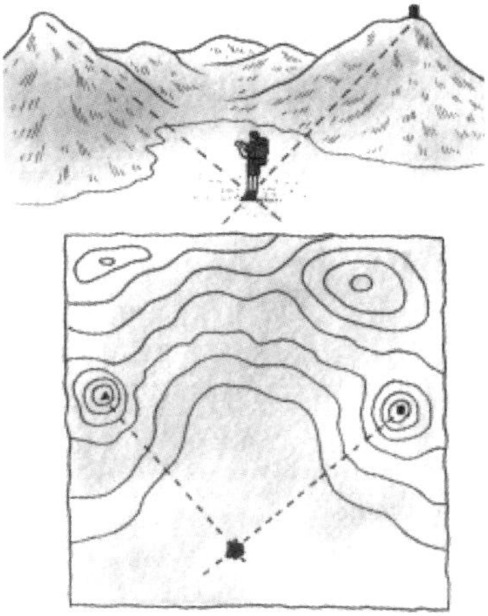

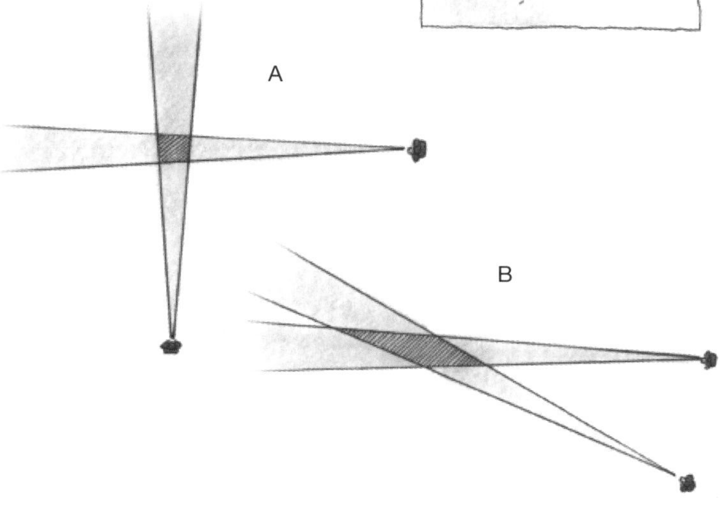

A

B

Prior knowledge is a major asset for any soldier trying to navigate his way to safety. Before any deployment, you should spend time learning the geography of your destination. The types of features you need to note include:

- The location of any substantial rivers in the region, and the direction in which they are flowing.
- The orientation of major physical features such as mountain ranges, glaciers or valleys.
- Which countries border the country to which you are being deployed, and the distances between those borders and major cities.
- The precise locations of military bases (friendly or otherwise) or territories known to be enemy strongholds.
- The direction of prevailing winds.
- Stars visible in the night sky at any particular time of year.
- The nature of the terrain across the region, noting places that are unsuitable for human travel.

This knowledge can make all the difference to your ability to navigate through the wilderness. For example, you might know that to reach a particular border area you need to keep a specific mountain range on your right-hand side, and a major river to your left.

The most useful device an evader can possess is a magnetic compass. A compass can work in all weathers, doesn't run out of batteries and if properly used will help you to maintain a consistent bearing. If a professional compass isn't available, you can make a crude improvised version out of some basic materials – see the box opposite. Some compasses made in POW camps reached surprising levels of sophistication. One prisoner of Stalag Luft III, Oliver Philpot, made a floating compass complete with directional bezel and fluorescent needle from a razor blade, parts of a gramophone, pieces of cardboard and phosphorous-coated hands from broken watches.

When you have decided upon a bearing, keep checking it regularly, but make sure that your compass is kept away from magnetic influences such as radio equipment and car engines, which could produce a false north reading. An improvised compass will have its limits, and the navigation won't have finer grades of accuracy, but it will help you keep travelling in roughly the right direction.

Natural navigation

Another aid to navigation is nature itself. The value of natural features in this regard can vary considerably depending on the season and the weather, but they have been used successfully by navigators for

US Army Tip: Making a Compass

You can construct improvised compasses using a piece of ferrous metal that can be needle-shaped or a flat double-edged razor blade, and a piece of nonmetallic string or long hair from which to suspend it. You can magnetize or polarize the metal by slowly stroking it in one direction on a piece of silk or carefully through your hair using deliberate strokes. You can also polarize metal by stroking it repeatedly at one end with a magnet. Always rub in one direction only. If you have a battery and some electric wire, you can polarize the metal electrically. The wire should be insulated. If not insulated, wrap the metal object in a single, thin strip of paper to prevent contact. The battery must be a minimum of 2 volts. Form a coil with the electric wire and touch its ends to the battery's terminals. Repeatedly insert one end of the metal object in and out of the coil. The needle will become an electromagnet. When suspended from a piece of nonmetallic string, or floated on a small piece of wood in water, it will align itself with a north-south line.

– FM 21–76, *US Army Survival Manual* (1992)

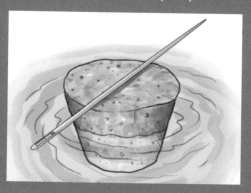

Navigation by Shadow

Shadow navigation is an ancient, but accurate, method of finding an east–west line, and therefore a north–south line. Find a shade stick that casts a shadow several feet long – this will give you a decent angle to work with after about 30 minutes' duration. For more details, see below.

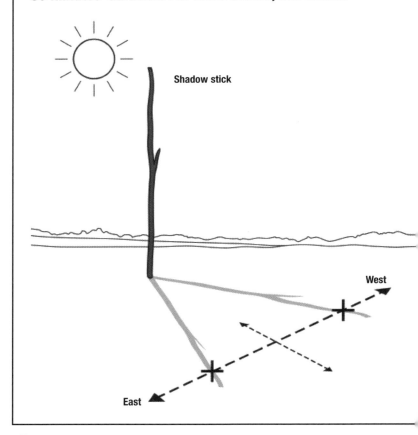

Shadow stick

West

East

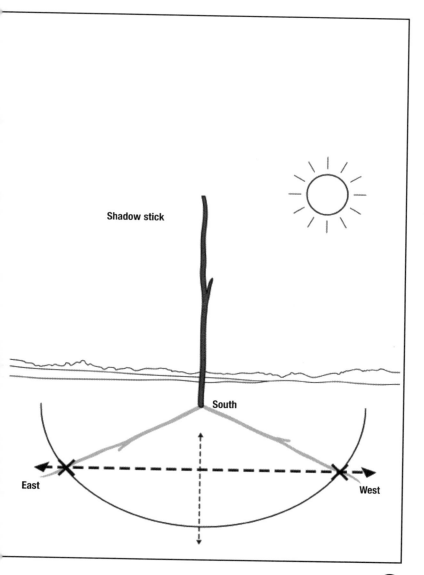

Shadow stick

South

East

West

centuries. In the daytime, and on a clear day, the sun provides a massive celestial navigation tool by rising predictably in the east and setting in the west. At midday in the Northern Hemisphere the sun is due south, and due north in the Southern Hemisphere. (If you are almost on the Equator, the midday sun will be straight above you.)

A classic tool for sun navigation is a shadow compass, made with nothing more than a stick and a few rocks. First, push a long stick into a patch of flat, even ground so that it stands vertically about 1m (3ft) above the earth (the longer the stick, the better the results). Under direct sunlight, the stick will throw a dark shadow onto the ground. Mark the tip of the shadow with a stone and wait about 30 minutes, during which time the shadow will move as the sun travels further across the sky. Mark the tip of the shadow again with another stone, then scrape a straight mark in the soil between the two stones and you have your east–west line. Bisecting this line will give you north–south orientation. Repeating this process at regular intervals can help you maintain a specific bearing, and to avoid aimless wandering.

You can also use an analogue watch (i.e. one with hands) for sun navigation. First set the watch to true local time – do not incorporate any daylight-saving additions or subtractions. Now hold the watch face flat, with the sun visible. In the Northern Hemisphere, point the hour hand towards the sun and bisect the angle between the hour hand and the 12 o'clock mark on the watch face. This direction is south, except before 06:00 and after 18:00, when it will indicate north. To make a reading in the Southern Hemisphere, point the 12 o'clock mark itself at the sun, and then bisect the angle between the mark and the hour hand to find north, or south before 06:00 and after 18:00. If you have a digital watch, simply draw out an analogue representation of the time on a piece of paper or the ground, and make the same calculation.

As an evader, much of your movement may well be made at night. Here also, there are age-old opportunities for celestial navigation, although any sort of cloud cover can unhelpfully obscure the stars. In the Northern Hemisphere, the North Star or Polaris is the most dependable heavenly body for guiding your navigation, as its position in the sky does not change. (See the illustration below for how to find Polaris using the Big Dipper/Plough and Cassiopeia constellations.)

By locating Polaris, you can either follow it directly or choose another star on the bearing you want and follow that instead. If you do the latter, refresh your course every 20–30 minutes, as other stars are rotating around the Pole Star at 15°

Watch Navigation

Watch navigation (see text opposite for details) depends on your having an analogue watch (one with hands). If you have a digital watch, however, simply draw a clock face and the correct time on a piece of paper, and use this.

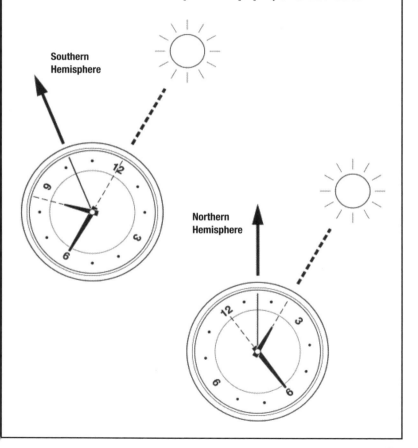

Southern
Hemisphere

Northern
Hemisphere

Pole Star/Polaris

Polaris can be located by using the Plough or Cassiopeia star formations as shown. Polaris rests unerringly in the north, so can be used either as a point of travel or as a star from which you can maintain a bearing as you travel. Cloud cover obviously removes the stars as a navigation source, so note natural ground features aligned with your direction of travel while the stars are visible.

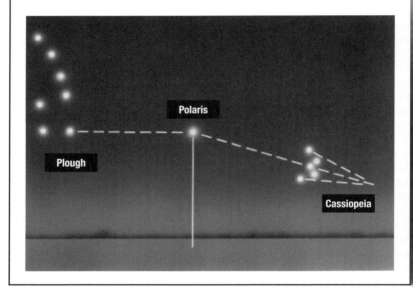

per hour. Keep selecting new stars to guide you on the right course. Another useful Northern Hemisphere constellation is Orion, which has a straight 'belt' of three stars spaced evenly in a straight line. Orion rises almost exactly due east and sets almost exactly due west, and the three stars run on an east–west alignment. As Orion sets below the horizon, the point at which the belt disappears out of sight is due west.

For those in the Southern Hemisphere, the Southern Cross provides clear guidance – when it is standing vertically in the sky, south is directly below the bottom star. If the Cross is at an angle, multiply the longest axis of the cross by 4.5, which brings you to an imaginary point above the horizon. Direct south will be immediately below the point.

Plants and terrain

Navigation using the sun and stars can be surprisingly accurate, but there are many times when the weather negates their use. In these instances, there are other natural features and elements that can provide directional guidance, albeit very general. The direction of prevailing winds, for example, is often indicated by trees and bushes bent in a common direction, particularly around coastal areas, or snowfalls or sand dunes sculpted into regular patterns. Transverse dunes, which occur in areas of deep sand, set themselves perpendicular to the wind, with a long, gentle slope facing into the wind, and a steep downwind slope. In arid areas with thin sand, the dunes tend to present themselves parallel to the prevailing wind.

Plants can also give directional hints. Plants and trees tend to grow most luxuriously towards the south (in the Northern Hemisphere) or north (in the Southern Hemisphere), the direction from which comes the

Star Orientation

If you can't find a particular star or constellation in the sky, any star can provide you with navigational information. For this exercise, you need to sit still for about 15 to 20 minutes. Note two fixed points on the ground in the distance, then pick a star and monitor its movement in relation to these points. The direction of the star will, according to the following rules, tell you in which direction you are facing:

Northern Hemisphere:
Rising – the star is in the east
Falling – the star is in the west
Left – the star is in the north
Right – the star is in the south

Southern Hemisphere:
Rising – the star is in the west
Falling – the star is in the east
Left – the star is in the south
Right – the star is in the north

strongest sunlight. Similarly, in the Northern Hemisphere mountains generally display more vegetation on the lower slopes of their southern faces. (Note also that in springtime the north-facing slopes are usually the last ones to keep the remnants of winter snow and ice.) The reverse principles are true in the Southern Hemisphere.

As with all natural navigation, however, be careful when reading plant signs. Many factors affect plant growth, including soil conditions and competition from surrounding flora, so they are a fallible method of navigation. Used in combination with other natural signs, however, they can be useful for adding to your sense of direction.

Communications and Signalling

Establishing radio communications with friendly forces is undoubtedly a major step towards your eventual recovery, depending on whether you have a radio in the first place. Once you can communicate with your own side, then you can cooperate effectively in either recovery operations or your safe passage through the frontlines. Many professional military survival radios will also feature a locator beacon, to give the receiver a precise fix on your position.

The danger of establishing radio communications is quite simply that the enemy might be listening; in fact, it is safe to assume that he is. Careless or excessive radio transmissions, therefore, can actually do more harm than good.

Not only might they endanger you by giving away your position, but they could also threaten the recovery team, by leading them directly into an enemy ambush. Furthermore, you will have only limited battery life in your radio. Your evasion action could last days or even weeks, which means that you cannot afford to waste a single minute of air time.

The following are the key rules for what the US military terms 'Electronic Counter-Countermeasures' (ECCM), which is simply the practice of avoiding electronic detection:

Minimize transmissions

Keep radio transmissions to a bare minimum in both volume and duration, speaking infrequently and only then to convey and receive absolutely essential information. Don't make idle chat, and pre-plan the transmissions beforehand so you speak with maximum efficiency (3–5 seconds for each transmission at most).

If the feature is available on your radio handset, use data burst transmissions (a system whereby Morse messages are compressed and broadcast at ultra-fast speeds).

Satellite Phone

A survival satellite phone is an expensive piece of kit, but it will give more dependable communication than a cell phone when you are in particularly remote areas. If you do use a cell phone, it has to be configured for the international roaming or the local networks.

Mask the transmissions

To minimize the risk of enemy radio interception, use the radio on a low-power setting and ideally with a directional antenna facing towards the recovery asset in a clear line-of-sight (LOS) arrangement. Make the broadcasts from a concealed position, with terrain features masking the signal either side of the LOS. If you don't know the direction of the recovery forces, focus your LOS towards the Equator.

Confuse the enemy

In a combat zone, once you have made a transmission you should move location, so the enemy struggles to gain a decent fix on your position. Use any pre-agreed codewords to make your transmission more incomprehensible to the enemy, and demand authentication codes from any reciprocal radio traffic – make sure that the person on the other end is who he says he is. Use encryption if the means of doing so is available on your radio, and if you have the technical know-how to transmit through decoy antennas to mask your real location.

If you do establish communications, you have to agree to a viable rescue plan and recovery location. These elements are discussed in more detail below. However, a real-life example of survival communications is beneficial here. We return to the story of Scott O'Grady, the US airman shot down over Yugoslavia in 1995. As he evaded Serbian forces, it was imperative that he make contact with US rescue forces.

The most critical piece of equipment he had in his F-16's survival pack was a small PRC-112 survival radio, capable of seven hours' broadcasting, and with locating beacon, Morse and voice transmission capabilities.

As well as evading the enemy, O'Grady searched for a high place suitable for both effective radio transmissions and safe extraction, and some five days after he was first shot down he managed to make contact with US electronic surveillance aircraft using the locator beep function.

This precipitated a massive US air response, as both combat and reconnaissance aircraft swarmed over the area. Finally, O'Grady made a voice connection with an overhead F-16, simply stating 'Basher-52 reads you. I'm alive, help.' The F-16 pilot replied, asking O'Grady an authentication question. This short conversation, of a very disciplined nature despite the emotion of the moment, was enough to set in train the rescue operation, about which we say more below.

Of course, a device available to many evaders is a mobile phone. If you have a signal, then you can use the phone to make contact with

Radio Strength

The strength of a radio signal varies with the orientation of the user. It is at its strongest when the operator is in a direct line of sight with the receiver, and it progressively weakens as the angle widens.

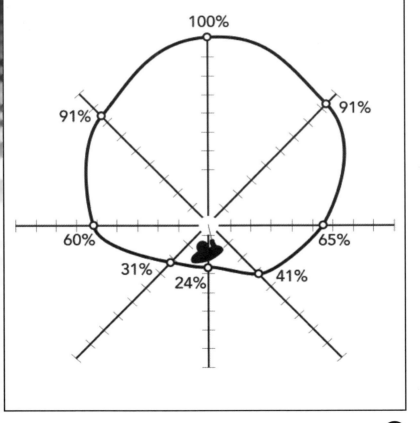

anyone who can initiate a rescue procedure. Cell phone conversations are easily intercepted, unless the phone is of a secured type, so obey all the transmission protocols above and use the phone only in an absolute crisis.

A new generation of what are now called 'Military Smart Phones' have also started to include features of real value to an evader. These include GPS navigation, real-time troop position maps, encrypted messaging and downloadable UAV video, which may give evaders crucial advantages over less technically advanced enemies.

Improvised signalling

Many military personnel on evasion will not have the luxury of a radio with them. In these cases, the best way to attract rescue is by signalling.

The keys to successful signalling are location and method. In terms of location, you ideally want to signal from a place in which you have LOS with friendly forces, but are shielded from enemy view. Admittedly, such a position is not always possible. In this case you can either select a method of signalling that can be controlled in terms of direction, or signal only when you expect a rescue mission will reach you before the enemy does.

Often the object of signalling is to attract the attention of overhead reconnaissance or combat aircraft,

Morse Code

The advantage of morse code is that it can be transmitted by means both visual (e.g. torch flashes) and auditory (e.g. whistle). Obviously it is not securely encoded, although some sophisticated radios can transmit a recorded morse message as a lightning-fast burst transmission.

A . ▬

B ▬ . . .

C ▬ . ▬ .

D ▬ . .

E .

F . . ▬ .

G ▬ ▬ .

H . . . .

I ..	W .__
J .___	X _.._
K _._	Y _.__
L ._..	Z __.._
M __	1 .____
N _.	2 ..___
O ___	3 ...__
P .__.	4 ...._
Q __._	5 .....
R ._.	6 _....
S ...	7 __...
T _	8 ___..
U .._	9 ____.
V ..._	0 _____

Ground-to-air Signals

Ground-to-air signals need to be built on a fairly grand scale to be seen from an overflying aircraft. They should also contrast with the natural background as well – for example, a signal made from rocks will stand out better on a grassy floor than a signal made from leafy branches.

Need doctor

Need signal lamp

Require medical assistance

Require food and water

Require assistance

Need map/compass

Need signal lamp

Indicates direction to proceed

Moving this direction

Will try to take off

Aircraft damaged

Safe to land

Need fuel/oil

All is well

No

Yes

Not understood

Require engineer

which might be out looking for you anyway. One way you can make contact is by creating ground-to-air signals. These are large emblems, mapped out on the ground, which are visible to overflying aircraft and which have an internationally recognized meaning.

You can create the signals from manmade materials such as parachute fabric or space blankets, or from natural materials such as tree branches, piles of stones, mounds of snow or flattened grass.

The key is to make the emblem contrast as much as possible with its background, and to make the sign extremely large – about 5.5m (18ft) long at its greatest length. Also give the emblems clean angles and straight lines; such aren't present in nature, so stand out sharply.

The basic codes are as follows:

V = Require assistance.
X = Require medical assistance.
N = No/negative.
Y = Yes/affirmative.
h = Proceeding in this direction.

Mirror signalling

In addition to ground signals, two excellent methods of attracting attention – if you don't have professional pyrotechnics, that is – are mirror signalling and fire/smoke signals. Signalling mirrors are particularly powerful when used on bright, sunny days – tests have demonstrated that a flash of bright sunshine from a mirror can be seen for distances of more than 32km (20 miles) in the right conditions. The best device for this purpose is a professional heliograph, but any bright, metallic and reflective surface will work, such as a polished piece of metal or even the shiny side of a CD/DVD.

To use a basic signalling mirror, first catch the sunlight on it, and direct it onto the ground in front of you. Look at your target (say a rescue party or distant aircraft). Now move the patch of light up from the ground to point directly at the target. Create a flashing pattern of signals rather than a constant beam of light; the blinking flash will attract more attention at distance, and doesn't require you to be so accurate with your signalling.

Another method of using the signalling mirror is to hold it in one hand near your face, with your other hand outstretched in front of you and aimed at the target like a gunsight. Illuminate the back of this hand with the light from the mirror, then drop the hand so that the beam continues out to the target, waggling the mirror a bit to create the flashing pattern.

A good-quality or powerful torch can take the place of a reflector if available, but make sure that you have a clear signalling objective before you use up some of the power in your precious batteries.

Signalling Mirror

A signalling mirror can project a powerful flash of light over many miles distance. Here the user 'aims' the beam by pointing his left hand at the target, illuminating the palm of that hand with the reflected sunlight, then moving the hand in an up and down motion across the face of the mirror, producing a flashing signal.

Heliograph Signal

The heliograph is a more advanced signalling mirror. The user knows when the mirror is catching the sunlight because a beam of light falls through the hole in the centre of the heliograph onto the palm of his hand. Then the mirror is flashed towards the target aircraft.

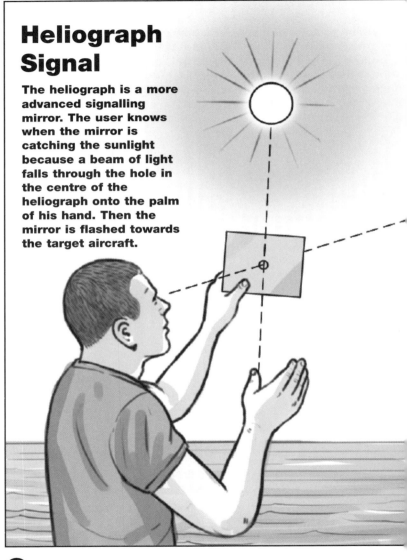

Signal fires

A less-sophisticated but even more effective way of attracting attention is a signal fire. Signal fires come in two main types. During the daytime, you want to create a smoky fire, with the colour of the smoke contrasting sharply with the background. To create dark smoke, add materials like tyres, plastics or petroleum products; for white smoke, add green, leafy vegetation. At night, by contrast, you need a signal fire that blazes brightly in the darkness.

As we have seen previously, making a fire from scratch is not a spur-of-the-moment activity, and it is unlikely that you can make one quickly enough to catch the attention of a passing aircraft. An alternative option is to have a fire ready-built but not lit in an area that is likely to see friendly aircraft traffic. Ideally, the construction should be treated with a fire accelerant such as petrol or munitions propellant, so it can be ignited the instant you spot an aircraft. Be careful when igniting such a fire, however, as the accelerant can create an explosion type effect when it initially catches fire.

Whatever your means of making contact, once you have gained the attention of friendly forces, and they have identified both you and your location, then it is time for the rescue to begin. Obviously be vigilant for enemy forces, who might also have spotted your signalling.

Building a Signal Fire

A signal fire requires plenty of dry, combustible materials that will catch fire quickly, plus lots of air gaps to encourage heat and flames. Here dry grasses and branches are piled on top of an open wood framework.

Tree Signal

If you don't have time to prepare a signal fire, another option is simply to set fire to a prominent tree. Make sure the tree is isolated from surrounding trees, or you are likely to start a forest fire.

Recovery

Many recovery operations in modern warfare are conducted by aerial means, typically a mixed force of rescue/special forces helicopters (to make the actual extraction) and fixed-wing combat and reconnaissance aircraft to provide security over the extraction site.

Landing zone

You need to find a suitable landing zone (LZ) for the helicopters, one on which a helicopter can either land safely or hover close to the ground and lower down a hoist recovery device. A good LZ is typically 45m (150ft) in diameter, with a flat, level surface and free from dangerous obstructions such as trees and large rocks. Around its perimeter, or nearby, you should have access to several places of concealment, so you can keep yourself hidden until the rescue is imminent.

You should also plan for what to do if the rescue mission is aborted, noting safe routes by which you can slip away from the LZ. Maintain communication with the rescue party throughout, warning them of approaching dangers such as enemy forces moving into the area.

During the actual recovery phase, adopt a non-threatening posture and follow the rescue crew's instructions to the letter. Tie down any loose equipment that could be blown around by the helicopter's downdraft.

Don't approach the helicopter until told to do so, and stay clear of all rotors. Once aboard, make sure you are fastened in securely, and then enjoy the ride home. If the recovery is conducted from a hovering helicopter using a hoist recovery device, the procedure is somewhat different – see the feature box.

In the case of Scott O'Grady, once he had made contact with US forces just before midnight on 8 June 1995, a rapid rescue plan was put into action, courtesy of the 24th Marine Expeditionary Unit. Two Sea Stallion helicopters from the USS *Kearsarge*, carrying 51 Marines, were the principal rescue force, but total air assets involved numbered some 40 aircraft, including a heavy combat presence.

The helicopters arrived over the recovery area just after daybreak on 9 June, honing in on the locator beacon. O'Grady then ignited a yellow signal flare to indicate his position. The first Sea Stallion landed, and 20 Marines sprang out to establish a security perimeter. The second helicopter then touched down, and its crew spotted O'Grady running towards them, through the early-morning fog. The side door was flung open, and within seven minutes of landing the helicopters were airborne again, with O'Grady heading to safety. It was a textbook rescue, and the culmination of an equally textbook evasion.

Using a Hoist

A rescue hoist lowered by a helicopter is first passed over your head (A) and fitted securely around your waist (B). Then cross your arms across the front of your torso (C), and grip on tight as you are hoisted into the air (D).

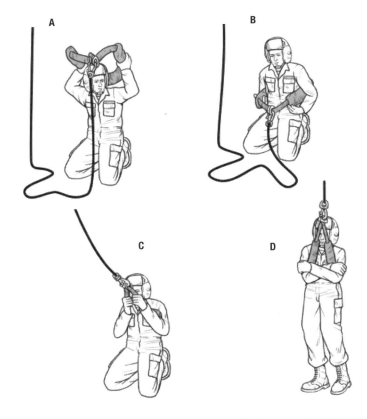

A

B

C

D

Helicopter Landing Zone

Helicopters require open spaces in which to land either vertically or by an oblique approach. Make sure that the helicopter can touch down with plenty of clearance between its rotor blades and high-standing obstacles – the diagrams here give the ideal dimensions for a wilderness landing zone.

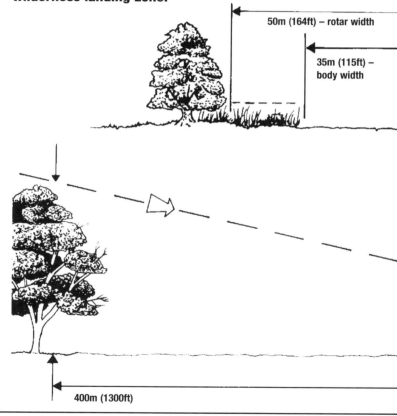

50m (164ft) – rotor width

35m (115ft) – body width

400m (1300ft)

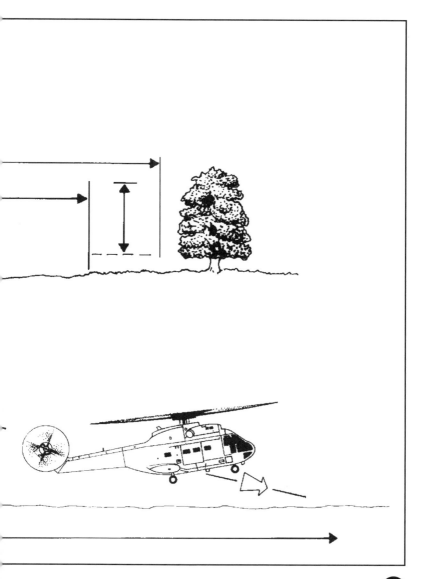

US Army Tip: Using a Hoist Recovery Device

For hoist recovery devices
(1) Use eye protection, if available (glasses or helmet visor).
(2) Allow metal on device to contact the surface before touching, to avoid injury from static discharge.
(3) Sit or kneel for stability while donning device.
(4) Put safety strap under armpits.
(5) Ensure cable is in front of you.
(6) Keep hands clear of all hardware and connectors.

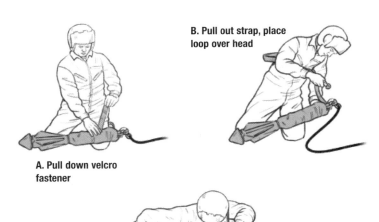

B. Pull out strap, place loop over head

A. Pull down velcro fastener

C. Fold down seat

(7) **DO NOT** become entangled in cable.
(8) Use a thumbs up, vigorous cable shake, or radio call to signal you are ready.
(9) Drag feet on the ground to decrease oscillation.
(10) **DO NOT** assist during hoist or when pulled into the rescue vehicle. Follow crewmember instructions.
– Air Land Sea Application Center, *Survival, Evasion, and Recovery* (1999)

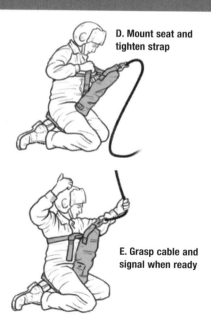

D. Mount seat and tighten strap

E. Grasp cable and signal when ready

F. Fold arms around device

Borders and Frontlines

Another option for reaching safety, already noted, is either to cross a border into a neutral or friendly country, or pass back through your own frontlines. Both approaches have significant risks. Border areas, particularly those separating combatants or suspicious neighbours, are often extremely well-protected, and border guards might respond with substantial force towards anyone trying to breach the border illegally.

This problem is even more acute around frontlines. Combat soldiers can be extremely jumpy on frontline areas, as they are more prepared for enemy infiltration than for POWs attempting to make safe passage. In such situations, you could easily end up being the victim of friendly fire.

Crossing Borders

When planning to cross over a border, make sure the country you are passing into will be friendly in the first place. Even if a state is not a combatant in the war you are fighting, it might well have international treaties that oblige it to return POWs, or even regard you as a hostile. As always, prior research pays off – discover as much as you can about the politics, culture and society of all the countries surrounding your area of deployment. Your goal should be to cross the border area safely, turn yourself into

the local authorities, and obtain contact with your consulate as soon as possible. Be compliant and informative in dealing with local authorities, but state clearly your rights as a foreign national and your need to make local contact.

Crossing a border is a delicate process. The safest way is to pass into another country through a relatively remote and unsecured area, where troop and border guard presence is minimal. Such areas, however, can be dangerous in terms of either terrain (treacherous geographical features sometimes demarcate unsecured border zones) or from banditry and crime, so move carefully.

If you choose to pass directly through a defended and fenced border zone, you are likely to face hi-tech challenges. Modern border security fences often include features such as seismic detectors, motion detectors, motion-activated lighting and flare launch systems, electrified wires and sensors to detect when wire has been cut, plus the presence of guards and dogs.

Prior reconnaissance is essential – choose to breach an area with a light guard presence and less formidable defences. Approach the border under the cover of darkness and preferably bad weather; on such nights the guards might become complacent from numerous false alarms, triggered by debris, rain and wind.

Approaching the Border

A border crossing is a dangerous moment for any evader. The challenge is that there can be security on both sides of the border, and trigger fingers can be especially twitchy around politically or militarily sensitive zones. Night crossings in areas of low security are recommended, even if it means travelling further.

Most decent security fences have anti-cut alarms, so simply cutting a hole through the wire threatens an immediate response.

Far better to go underneath the wire, holding it up carefully with a non-metallic rod. If the wire goes into the ground, try to dig a channel beneath it and then wriggle underneath on your back.

If going underneath isn't an option, then climbing over might be the only choice, although keep parallel to the wire to maintain a low profile. Once you are across, try to get away from the immediate border area and turn yourself in at a local police station or other official building.

Crossing Frontlines

Crossing combat frontlines adds even greater degrees of risk. The quandary is that the more covert you try to make the crossing, the greater the chance of your own side confusing you for an enemy if you are detected. If you make yourself too conspicuous, however, you will attract enemy attention.

As with crossing border zones, try to find an area that is poorly defended, or where threat levels are low and troops are less likely to open fire as a matter of course. Utilize your knowledge of your own side's security arrangements and systems, and their rules of engagement (ROE), to approach to within visual and auditory range of friendly positions. Then

announce your presence, stating your name, rank and unit but staying under cover in case a jittery soldier opens fire. The soldiers facing you are likely to be extremely cautious, so provide them with all requested information before showing yourself, with your hands raised high. Put down or shoulder any weapons you are carrying, thus lowering the levels of tension. When ordered to do so, approach slowly and methodically and give yourself up.

One additional danger you might face on the frontlines is that of minefields. These should be marked and are best avoided altogether. If you simply can't avoid going through a minefield, then you will have to practice basic methods of mine detection, using a mine probe. A mine probe is a slender, non-metallic and strong shaft of material, spiked at one end, which you push carefully into the ground to detect mines. The procedure for doing this is explained in the feature box, but mine probing is mentally and physically exhausting, and grindingly slow. It is far safer to select another route.

After Release

A successful escape and evasion is undoubtedly a cause for celebration. Yet the experience of sudden freedom is not always straightforward. Many former evaders or escaped POWs suffer from the legacies of post-traumatic stress

Crossing Wire

It is often better to cross under wire than over it. First dig a channel beneath the wire, wide enough to accommodate your body, then wriggle through the channel, holding the wire up with a non-conducting piece of material.

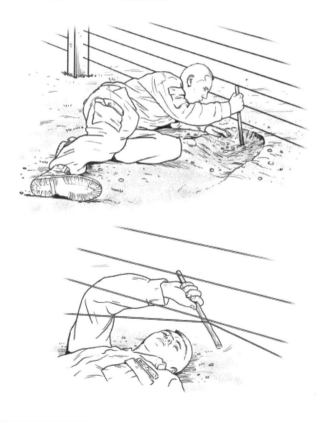

US Army Engineers Tips – Manual Mine Clearance

Physical detection (probing) is very time-consuming and is used primarily for mine-clearing operations and self-extraction. Detection of mines by visual or electronic methods should be confirmed by probing. Use the following procedures and techniques when probing for mines:

- Roll up your sleeves and remove your jewelry to increase sensitivity. Wear a Kevlar helmet, with the chin strap buckled, and a protective fragmentation vest.
- Stay close to the ground and move in a prone position to reduce the effects of an accidental blast. When moving into a prone position –
  - Squat down without touching your knees to the ground.
  - Scan forward up to 2 meters [6ft] and to the sides up to 3 meters [9ft] for mine indicators.
  - Probe the area around your feet and as far forward as possible.
  - Kneel on the ground after the area is found to be clear, and continue probing forward until you are in a prone position.
- Use sight and touch to detect trip wires, fuses, and pressure prongs.
- Use a slender, nonmetallic object as a probe.
- Probe every 5 centimeters [2in] across a 1-meter [3ft] front.
- Push the probe into the ground gently at an angle that is less than 45°.
- Apply just enough pressure on the probe to sink it slowly into the ground.
- Pick the soil away carefully with the tip of the probe. Remove the loose dirt by hand if the probe encounters resistance and does not go into the ground freely. Take care to prevent detonating the mine.
- Stop probing and use two fingers from each hand to carefully remove the surrounding soil when a solid object is touched and identify the object.
- Remove enough soil to show the mine type (if the object is a mine)

and mark its location. Do not attempt to remove or disarm the mine. Use explosives to destroy detected mines in place or use a grappling hook and rope to cause mines to self-detonate. Do not use metal grappling hooks on magnetic-fused mines.

– US Army, FM 3-34-2, *Combined-Arms Breaching Operations* (2001)

Crossing Frontlines

When approaching a frontline area, make yourself as unthreatening as possible. Hold your hands up and away from your body, and if you are holding a weapon put it down slowly on the floor, making no sudden movements. Comply with all orders to the letter.

disorder (PTSD), or from physical injuries sustained either in captivity or on the run. These must be treated immediately by professionals, to avoid serious long-term complications. The return to safety will also require extensive debriefing, plus caution about what you say publicly (see box below).

The essence of the USMC advice here is to remember that although you are free, others might still be in captivity. You can help future generations of warriors, however, by imparting your experience to others within the military community.

US Marine Corps Tip – Debriefing Escapees

The following is official USMC advice on coping with life once freed from a hostage situation, but it holds true for all escaped POWs:

Once you are safely in the hands of the authorities, remember to cooperate fully with them, especially if others are still being held. As soon as you can, write down everything you can remember: guard location, weapons and explosives description and placement, and any other information that might help rescue forces. After your release, you must prepare yourself for the aftermath. The news media will want an interview immediately, and you will be in no condition to provide intelligent, accurate responses. Do not make comments to the news media until you have been debriefed by proper U.S. authorities and have been cleared to do so by the appropriate military commanders. You should only say that you are grateful to be alive and thankful for being released. You should not say anything that could harm fellow hostages who may still be in captivity. You must not say anything that is sympathetic to the terrorist cause or that might gain support for them.

– MCRP 3-02E, *The Individual's Guide for Understanding and Surviving Terrorism* (2001)

BIBLIOGRAPHY

AFM 64-5, *Survival*. Boulder, Colorado: Paladin Press (1979)

CJCS, *Antiterrorism Personal Protection Guide: A Self-Help Guide to Terrorism*.
USA: Chairman of the Joint Chiefs of Staff (2002)

Dach Bern, von, Major H., *Total Resistance*. Boulder, Colorado: Panther Publications (1965)

Fowler, William, *Operation Barras: the SAS Rescue Mission, Sierra Leone 2000*.
London: Weidenfeld & Nicolson (2004)

FM 21-77, *Escape and Evasion*. USA: HQ Department of the Army (1958)

FM 7-93, *Long Range Surveillance Unit Operations*. USA: HQ Department of the Army (1995)

Mears, Ray, *Essential Bushcraft*. London: Hodder & Stoughton (2002)

Canadian Government, *Never Say Die: the Canadian Air Force Survival Manual*.
Boulder, Colorado: Paladin Press (1982)

Reid, Pat (MBE, MC), *Prisoner of War*. London: Hamlyn (1984)

Toliver, Raymond, *The Interrogator*. Fallbrook, USA, Aero Publishers (1978)

USMC, *Individual's Guide for Understanding and Surviving Terrorism*. USA: US Marine Corps
(2001)

Air Land Sea Application Center, *Survival, Evasion and Recovery*. USA: Air Land and Sea
Application Center (1999)

Wiseman, John, *SAS Survival Handbook*. London: HarperCollins (1986)

USEFUL WEBSITES

The US Fighting Man's Code:
www.loc.gov/rr/frd/Military_Law/pdf/US-fighting-code-1955.pdf

Code of the US Fighting Force: www.armypubs.army.mil/epubs/pdf/p360_512.pdf

US Military Field Manuals: www.globalsecurity.org/military/library/policy/army/fm/

USAF Air Rescue Service: www.airrescuemuseum.org

Wilderness Survival: www.wilderness-survival.net

Hostage Survival Skills for CF personnel: www.nato.int/docu/colloq/w970707/p6.pdf

GLOSSARY

ABC – a mnemonic for remembering immediate first aid priorities: Airway, Breathing, Circulation.

bearing – the compass direction from your position to a landmark or destination.

bergen – a large backpack for carrying survival supplies.

bivi-bag – a portable low-profile, one-man tunnel tent.

bola – a weapon consisting of multiple weights bound together by rope and thrown to bring down prey.

calorie – the amount of heat required to raise the temperature of 1 gram of water by 1° Celsius.

carbohydrate – an organic compound of carbon, hydrogen and oxygen found in many foods. When ingested, carbohydrates are broken down to provide energy.

circulatory shock – a medical emergency caused by a casualty's blood pressure dropping below safe levels.

collateral damage – damage not planned or expected to occur, e.g., civilian casualties in military operations, or an evader being caught up in fighting between two sides.

compromise – the capture of an escaped soldier, often resulting in return to captivity, further aggressive treatment and even death.

coniferous – denotes an evergreen tree with cones and needle-like leaves.

contour – a line on a map joining points of equal elevation.

coordinates – a pair of numbers and/or letters that describe a unique geographic position.

CPR – cardio-pulmonary resuscitation; a first aid term referring to methods of artificially maintaining blood circulation and breathing.

deadfall trap – a trap designed to kill an animal by dropping a heavy weight on it.

dehydration – in a person, a significant loss of body fluids that are not replaced by fluid intake.

dysentery – a chronic diarrhoeal illness that can lead to severe dehydration and, ultimately, death.

ECCM – Electronic Counter-Countermeasures; attempts to reduce the effect of electronic countermeasures by jamming or blocking electronic signals.

elevation – height above mean sea level.

ETO – European Theatre of Operations

fats – natural oily substances which, in humans, are derived from food and deposited in subcutaneous layers and around some major organs.

GPS – Global Positioning Satellite; refers to the navigational satellites orbiting the Earth, which a GPS receiver utilizes to determine its exact position of longitude and latitude.

grid – the horizontal and vertical lines on a map that enable you to describe position; on a map they have a north–south and east–west orientation.

grid reference – a position defined in relation to a cartographic grid.

hearth – in survival fire lighting, the piece of wood on which you generate heat sufficient to ignite tinder.

hyperthermia – a condition in which the body temperature rises to a dangerously high level. Also known as heat-stroke.

hypothermia – a condition in which the body temperature falls to a dangerously low level. Also known as exposure.

iodine – a chemical element that has a use in water purification.

IED – Improvised Explosive Device

insurgent – a person who militarily rebels against a political party or civil authority.

JDAM – Joint Direct Attack Munitions; a kit that converts a bomb with no guidance system into a precision-guided munition.

kindling – small pieces of dry material, usually thin twigs, added to ignited tinder to develop a fire.

layering – in survival clothing, refers to the principle of wearing multiple thin layers of clothing to control heat retention.

lure – anything used in fishing or hunting that tempts prey into a trap or particular location.

magnetic north – the direction of the magnetic North Pole.

monsoon – a period of intense rainfall and wind in India and Southeast Asia between May and September each year.

PTSD – Post-Traumatic Stress Disorder; a severe anxiety disorder, sometimes experienced by soldiers after psychologically traumatic events, such as capture or imprisonment.

potassium permanganate – a chemical that can be used to sterilize water.

RoE – Rules of Engagement, which address where, when, how and against whom military force can be used.

sign – a term used by trackers to denote any disturbance in the environment that indicates the previous passing of a human or animal.

smoking – the process of drying out food over a smoky fire, to increase the food's storage life.

solar still – a device that traps moisture from the soil under a plastic sheet, this condensing out into drinkable water.

stalking – in tracking, the art of moving silently and stealthily so as not to alert the quarry to your presence.

temperate – any climate characterized by mild temperatures.

tinder – small pieces of light and dry material that are very easily ignited and are used to initiate a fire.

track – a line of sign that indicates the route of an animal or human quarry through the environment.

tracking – the pursuit of an animal or human quarry by observing and following the sign they have left behind. See also sign.

transit – an imaginary straight line extended through two landmarks and used as a position line.

trench foot – also known as 'immersion foot'; a serious skin condition that results from prolonged exposure of feet to damp, cold and dirty conditions.

UET – Universal Edibility Test; a test to determine whether unidentified plants (not fungi) are safe for consumption.

vitamins – a group of organic compounds that are an essential part of human nutrition, though they are required in only very small doses.

Yukon stove – an advanced survival stove consisting of a chimney of mud-packed stones over a cooking pit.

INDEX